Understanding
Foucault

REFERENCE

Tony Schirato • Geoff Danaher • Jen Webb

Understanding Foucault

A critical introduction

2nd edition

Los Angeles | London | New Delhi
Singapore | Washington DC

© Tony Schirato, Geoff Danaher and Jen Webb 2012

First published 2012

First published in Australia by Allen & Unwin

SAGE Publications Ltd
1 Oliver's Yard
55 City Road
London EC1Y 1SP

SAGE Publications Inc.
2455 Teller Road
Thousand Oaks, California 91320

SAGE Publications India Pvt Ltd
B 1/I 1 Mohan Cooperative Industrial Are
Mathura Road
New Delhi 110 044

SAGE Publications Asia-Pacific Pte Ltd
33 Pekin Street #02-01
Far East Square
Singapore 048763

Library of Congress Control Number: 2011941383

British Library Cataloguing in Publication data

A catalogue record for this book is available from the British Library

ISBN 978-1-4462-5235-2 (pbk)

Typeset by Post Pre-Press Group, Australia
Printed in China at Everbest Printing Co.

10 9 8 7 6 5 4 3 2 1

MIX
Paper from responsible sources
FSC
www.fsc.org
FSC® C021256

The paper in this book is FSC® certified.
FSC® promotes environmentally responsible, socially beneficial and economically viable management of the world's forests.

Contents

Preface

Michel Foucault (1926–84) can be described as one of the most influential thinkers of our time. His work on power and institutional practices, discourse, subjectivity and sexuality has resonated throughout a diversity of academic fields such as philosophy, history, sociology, literary and cultural studies, psychology and theology, as well as shaping attitudes and practices beyond the academy. It is in terms of the breadth of this influence that Foucault can be distinguished from his French intellectual contemporaries such as Jacques Derrida and Gilles Deleuze, and his writing continues to inform the work of important contemporary scholars such as Judith Butler and Giorgio Agamben.

In response to the influence and usefulness of Foucault's ideas, a number of introductory texts have been published that take on the task of guiding readers through the complexities and implications of his thought. In the main these texts have focused on Foucault's major works, such as *Madness and Civilization*, *The Order of Things*, *The Archaeology of Knowledge*, *Discipline and Punish* and his three-volume *History of Sexuality*. At the same time, a number of biographical studies have been published that situate Foucault's work in the context of events that shaped both his own life and the world in which he lived, including World War II, his career within the French academy and his growing international reputation. While this book does not engage extensively with this biographical detail, it can be distinguished from other introductions by making considerable use not only of Foucault's books, but also of his lectures and other writings that have only been published in English in recent years. In particular, we draw upon the series of lectures Foucault presented each year as part of his role as Professor of the History of Systems of Thought at the Collège de France in Paris, a chair to which he was elected in 1970. They have been published under titles such as *Psychiatric Power* (the 1973–74 lectures), *Abnormal* (1974–75), *Society Must Be Defended* (1975–76), *Security, Territory, Population* (1977–78), *The Birth of Biopolitics* (1978–79), *The Hermeneutics of the Subject* (1981–82) and *The Government of Self and Others* (1982–83). These lectures constitute a particularly valuable addition to Foucault's corpus because of the insights they provide into the evolution and contexts of his ideas, along with shifts in the direction and emphasis of his thinking. Furthermore, they highlight the way in which all of Foucault's work, while it drew extensively from the historical record as far back as the Ancient Greeks, was focused on contemporary problems as they applied to people's everyday ideas, activities and subjectivities. Drawing upon these lectures and other recently published material has enabled us to build substantially upon our discussion of Foucault's work published in *Understanding Foucault* (2000).

We can help situate Foucault's ideas by considering them in relation to the various philosophies and bodies of knowledge he encountered throughout his intellectual career. In the years immediately following World War II, when Foucault was attending university and starting out as a scholar, there were two main bodies of theory and knowledge that dominated much of French intellectual life—Marxism and phenomenology. Marxism exerted a considerable influence, both politically and theoretically. These two areas—political commitment and activity on the one hand, and philosophy on the other—came together precisely because Marxism put itself forward as a philosophy that didn't just think or talk about the world. It wanted to change it, and finish off the 'march to freedom' that, for many French intellectuals, had begun with the French Revolution, by providing the theoretical tools through which the people could rise up and seize power from the property-owning class.

Phenomenology, particularly those theories of phenomenology that appeared in the work of Edmund Husserl and Martin Heidegger in Germany, and Maurice Merleau-Ponty in France, was also influential, theorising that all meaning was to be found in a person's perception of the 'universal essence' of an object or thing. This led to the 'existential philosophy' of Sartre, who posited the individual as more or less a free agent, both responsible for and capable of organising experience and making sense of it. From this perspective, all truth came out of the ability of human subjects to consider and understand what was going on around them, including their own involvement in the world—their desires, motivations and activities. In part, the influence of phenomenology and existentialism was a response to the moral crisis generated by World War II. In a world of such wanton mass slaughter, where it seemed impossible to believe in a higher meaning governed by a supreme being, it was up to individuals to decide how to live authentically.

For Foucault, Marxism and phenomenology were flawed theoretical models that relied upon unsustainable assumptions. Marxism offered a totalising vision that reduced all historical struggles to class-based conflict, and depended on a teleological view that posited a grand march of human progress towards the utopia where such conflict could be resolved in a classless society. Phenomenology depended on a similarly fixed and absolutist view of human subjectivity as constituting the foundation through which all experience could be made meaningful.

Foucault was instead interested in the ways in which all notions of truth, subjective meaning, knowledge and reason were shaped by historical forces. As such, early in his intellectual career he was influenced by the 'historicising' work of Martin Heidegger and the 'scientific histories' of Georges Canguilhem. Although Heidegger was a phenomenologist, he emphasised the centrality of the temporal contexts in which truth and meaning were produced. For Heidegger, ideas and activities were largely determined by the background in which they existed, but this relationship could never really be made clear—people tended to think that they were acting freely and independently of their contexts. Canguilhem's work was concerned with scientific ideas (particularly in the area of biology), but what really interested him was the way in which scientific rationality and reason were always changing, and the way that 'bodies of knowledge and truth', which were thought to be universal, could come to an end and be replaced by a different 'truth' or rationality.

What Foucault took from these two theorists was, first, the notion that what people could know was always limited by their contexts, and second—and relatedly—that what constituted truth and rationality was not inevitable (scientific 'breakthroughs', for instance, often happened by chance) and could change within and across history.

There were two other bodies of theory that influenced French intellectual life, including the work of Foucault, from the 1960s onwards—structuralism and psychoanalytical theory. Foucault was aware of the line of structuralist work stretching back to the early twentieth century, including Saussure and Jakobson (linguistics), Levi-Strauss, Boas and Dumezil (anthropology), the Russian formalists (linguistics and literature) and the Annales School of historians. Two other contemporary French theorists, Roland Barthes (literature and semiotics) and Louis Althusser (Marxism and political theory)—who was also one of Foucault's teachers—also exerted an influence on him. *The Order of Things* and *The Archaeology of Knowledge*, in particular, were read by some critics as structuralist works, though Foucault denied this.

In its focus on cultural systems such as language, or familial networks and practices, structuralism showed how meanings did not emerge from a founding subject, but were generated from one's place in a system and relationship with others. For example, a word like 'cat' can only make sense in terms of being different from 'dog', while the distinctions constructed between groups in a social structure on the basis of categories like gender, age and ethnicity have important implications for the lifestyles of those constructed in this way. Psychoanalytical theory—especially as developed through the works of Sigmund Freud and, later, Jacques Lacan—continued this critique of the 'free subject'. According to Freud and Lacan, the subject is a kind of myth that comes about when we repress our desires in order to be accepted into society. Lacan theorised that the subject could never know itself—its existence was based on a kind of necessary ignorance.

Although Foucault was influenced by these two bodies of theory, he rejected the notion that structuralist analysis could 'deliver up' the whole meaning of something—a book or a period of history—by analysing all its relevant 'relations', because this overlooked what was excluded from this system—specifically, what was repressed or impossible to think within the system. Furthermore, structuralism could not account for the historical shifts and discontinuities that wrought changes in these relations, nor could it account for the way in which individual actions and utterances negotiated and in some cases resisted the rules through which the system operated.

Foucault's problems with psychoanalysis centred on the point that while on the one hand it helped to do away with the notion of the 'knowing subject' by introducing the ideas of repression and the unconscious, on the other it claimed to understand and make sense of the 'truth' of the subject. For Foucault, psychoanalysis constituted another historical force that generated discourse, theories and practices through which particular notions of subjectivity and sexuality were constructed. In other words, rather than according theories like psychoanalysis, Marxism, phenomenology and structuralism a privileged position in terms of their being able to reveal the truth of one's inner nature or relations with others within a fixed system, Foucault wanted to explore the ways in which such theories were bound up in what they constructed, helping to constitute the conditions of possibility through which an individual and society is made sense of in a particular way.

One important influence for Foucault—particularly in terms of his theorising of power from the 1970s on—was the German philosopher Friedrich Nietzsche. Nietzsche rejected the notion that history unfolds in a rational way, with the gradual development of higher forms of reason. He rejected attempts to identify a historical point— say, Ancient Greece or Imperial Rome—as the origin of an essential idea, way of life or value (democracy, western civilisation, reason). In fact, any form of knowledge or truth that emerged in a culture did so, Nietzsche argued, not because it was valuable or eternal, but because one group had managed to naturalise one regime of value or meaning at the expense of another. Whereas Marxism could survey the field of history and come up with a single narrative, Nietzsche would insist that there were many possible stories and developments, but that these alternatives had to be repressed and forgotten so that dominant groups could justify the 'inevitability' of their own rise to power. Like Nietzsche, Foucault emphasised the importance of critique, which he understood both in terms of an investigation into what we are (how we think, what we value, how we understand ourselves, how we treat others) and as a concern with thinking what else we might be (how we could be different from ourselves).

Besides seeking to both draw from and distinguish his thinking from other theoretical perspectives, it is clear that his own experiences and domestic and international events shaped Foucault's work as an intellectual. The student protests in Paris in 1968, as well as Foucault's witnessing of student uprisings in Tunisia, were influential in challenging authorised ways of thinking both within the academy and beyond. Such events helped stir a number of French scholars, such as Gilles Deleuze, Michel de Certeau and Jacques Derrida—who collectively and somewhat misleadingly have been labelled post-structuralists.

What they shared was an interest in breaking open essences and unities in thought, rendering contingent what had tended to be taken for granted as normal and real. At the same time Foucault's active involvement in causes like prison reform demonstrated the practical application of his intellectual work, and helped to inform political and social struggles both within France and abroad. From the 1970s, Foucault's growing international reputation, and his travels to places like Japan and California, extended the range of his interests and involvement in particular causes. This coupling of critical intellectual work with a commitment to movements for social change, such as gay rights, has been a distinctive feature of Foucault's legacy.

Thus Foucault's own work can be understood within this sensibility of critique, which is aimed at challenging the forces that govern us, not only in a broad political sense but also in terms of the forms of language, apparatuses of power and other forces that shape how we think and act. This meant adopting a specifically historicising perspective in order to reveal the contingency of all claims to, and notions of, truth and knowledge. By drawing upon his major works, lecture series and other publications, this book will explore how Foucault conducted an ongoing experiment in thought that involved engaging with diverse historical events, ideas and social practices.

Just a brief explanatory note: in this Preface, which deals with Foucault's work and concepts in a general and contextual manner, we have used the term 'human' ('human progress', 'human subjectivity') where Foucault might have made use of the discursive category and term 'man'. When we are dealing more specifically with Foucault's discourse and texts, we will follow his usage of the term 'man'.

Acknowledgements

We would like to acknowledge and indicate our appreciation of the valuable contributions made by the following: Professor John Frow of the University of Melbourne; Elizabeth Weiss, Angela Handley, Sue Jarvis and Kate Goldsworthy from Allen & Unwin; Mila Steele from Sage; Dr Stephanie Rains, Professor Gavin Titley and administrative staff at the National University of Ireland at Maynooth; and staff at the Reading Room of the National Library of Ireland in Dublin.

Acknowledgements

Glossary of theoretical terms

Aphrodisia. Foucault translates this Greek concept, with clear difficulty and reservation, as pleasures of love or carnality (1986: 35). He suggests that *aphrodisia* is characterised by a dynamic relationship between desires, acts and pleasures—a relationship that suffers dissociation in the Christian period, when pleasure is simply left without a place in the largely procreation-based arrangement of sexuality.

Archaeology. The term used by Foucault to refer to the process of working through the historical archives of various societies to bring to light the discursive formations and events that have produced the fields of knowledge and discursive formations of different historical periods.

Askesis. From the Greeks, it refers to the notion of a regime of self-testing and training.

Biopolitics and biopower. Refer to the technologies, forms of knowledge, discourses, politics and practices used to bring about the production and management of a state's human resources.

Biopower analyses, regulates, controls, explains and defines the human subject, its body and behaviour.

Bodily hexis. The forms of bodies, and bodily movements and deportment, that are commensurate with, authorised by and appropriately reflect the values of a cultural field.

Carceral continuum. The idea that techniques of coercion and correction developed in the prison were carried through disciplinary power to other institutional sites, such as the school, workhouse and military barracks.

Care of the self. For Foucault, this refers both to the historical development of the notion of the cultivation of the self, and to the techniques and ethical regimes through which the care of the self is practised.

Critique and critical inquiry. A space opened up by the testing of reality in order to evaluate the possibility and desirability of change, and determine the forms it will take.

Cultural capital. Anything that has value and is exchangeable within a cultural field or fields. The production and acceptance of, and changes to, cultural capital are determined within and by specific fields.

Cultural field. A concept taken from Bourdieu; it can be defined as a set of institutions, rules, categories, discourses, dispositions, forms of capital and practices that forms an objective hierarchy, and that produces and authorises identities.

Delinquency. A mode of subjectivity defined in terms of its difference from the social norm: the properly moulded and temperate person. In prisons, delinquency can take the form of the recidivist offender who keeps refusing to conform to mechanisms of correction and training.

Descending individualism. Refers to the way in which, in modern western societies, people are more closely monitored and 'individualised' the lower on the social scale they are. Under the old order of feudal societies and monarchical rule, the more powerful one was, the more watched and noticed one became. 'Descending individualism' operates according to the opposite impulse: prisoners are monitored and individualised by guards, pupils by teachers, children by parents, patients by doctors and so on.

Desire. In psychoanalytic terms, this is something that is sent away or repressed in order that the subject can exist; however, repressed desire always returns without overtly manifesting or articulating itself—for instance, in dreams. Desire, for Nietzsche, is the will manifested as the affirmation of life-as-force. For Foucault, however, desire is first and foremost a name with a history—in other words, its status fundamentally is discursive.

Dialectical materialism. A concept derived from the philosophy of Karl Marx. Marx applied Hegel's concept of the dialectic, involving the struggle of opposing forces that might be resolved by the emergence of a new synthesis, to the material economic conditions of society. For Marx, the struggle between the bourgeois property-owning class and the proletariat working class in nineteenth-century Europe would eventually give rise to the emergence of a Communist utopian society.

Disciplinary institutions. Refers to institutions emerging in nineteenth-century Europe, such as prisons, workhouses, schools and barracks, which took hold of the bodies and minds of their inhabitants and shaped them according to disciplinary procedures and 'quiet coercions'.

Discipline. Refers first to the notion of punishment or coercion, and second to the notion of sets of skills and forms of knowledge that must be mastered in order to achieve success in particular fields. Foucault connects these two meanings through his concept of 'power–knowledge'.

Discourse. Generally refers to a type of language associated with and authorised by an institution or cultural field, which articulates the ideas and statements that express a particular set of values and a certain world-view. In Foucault's writings, it is used to describe individual acts of language, or 'language in action'—the ideas and statements that allow us to make sense of and 'see' things.

Dividing practices. Refers to the ways in which social groups are separated from one another on the basis of judgements made about their actions and attitudes—for example, the mad are divided from the sane, the sick from the healthy, the criminal from the legal.

Enlightenment. For Foucault, this is both a collection of ideas and attitudes (concerning reason, justice, equality, progress and rationality) and a series of political events (including the French Revolution). Historically, the Enlightenment sought to replace the old order of absolute sovereignty, injustice, ignorance and superstition with an order based on reason, rationality and equality. More specifically, Foucault understood the Enlightenment as being based on an interrogation of how and what and why things are, and as a particular self-referential attitude to oneself and one's time.

Episteme. A period of history organised around, and explicable in terms of, specific world-views and discourses. Epistemes are characterised and maintained by institutions, disciplines, forms of knowledge, rules and activities consistent with those world-views. The change from one episteme to another is not clearcut, nor does it correspond to any notion of natural continuity, development or progress, but rather is random and contingent.

Ethics. For Foucault, this term refers to how people behave in relation to 'moral' norms—understood as the sets of rules, prohibitions and codes of a society. It also refers to and presumes a necessary continuity between and across a set of discourses, narratives and practices.

Games of truth. Refers to the sets of rules within particular institutions by and through which different forms of truth are produced.

Genealogy. The process of analysing and uncovering the historical relationship between truth, knowledge and power. Foucault suggests, following Nietzsche, that knowledge and truth are produced by struggles both between and within institutions, fields and disciplines, and then presented as if they were eternal and universal.

Governance and government. For Foucault, these concepts can be understood both in terms of a 'body politics' (the ways in which we conduct ourselves, the relationships that we have with our body and other bodies in society) and, in a more conventional sense, the way in which a state rules over its people.

Governmentality. The term Foucault uses to describe the change in technologies of, and attitudes towards, governing that occurred in Europe in the eighteenth century. This involved a greater emphasis on the state's ability to manage its resources (including its population) economically and efficiently, and a concomitant increase in state intervention in the lives of its citizens. There have been two major consequences of this change. The first is that citizens are both 'regulated' by the state and its institutions and discourses, and educated to monitor and regulate their own behaviour. The second, which derives from what Foucault calls the 'liberal attitude', is the emergence of an understanding on the part of citizens of the need to 'negotiate' those forces of 'subject regulation' through a process of 'self-governing'.

Habitus. A term used by the French sociologist Pierre Bourdieu, which refers to the ways in which we are produced as subjects through sets of dispositions that predispose us to think and behave in ways adapted to the structures within which we are constituted. Since these are dispositions, they are embodied, durable and largely unconscious.

Hegemony. A term developed by the Marxist theorist Antonio Gramsci, which refers to the way in which states and state institutions work to produce popular consent for their authority through a variety of processes that disguise their position of dominance.

Heterotopia. Refers to the way in which radically different social spaces can come into connection with one another. For example, the space of the gentlemen's clubs that British colonists established in India was radically different from the social space through which the Indian people moved and made sense of their world.

History of sexuality. Foucault's work in this area can be characterised as bringing to light socio-cultural events that enable us to recognise power 'doing its work'—specifically the establishment, over a considerable period of history, of a particular kind of relationship between the subject and the notion of governmentality that culminates, from the eighteenth century onwards, in the modern subject of desire.

Human sciences (also known as social sciences). Constituted fields such as sociology, psychology, criminology, nursing, economics and linguistics. They encompassed disciplines and forms of knowledge that took 'man'—understood as a sovereign and self-originating subject, rather than just another living species—as their object of study, along with other factors that affected the human (space and architecture, for instance). These sciences differed from the natural sciences, according to Foucault, in not being generalised theories (say, about the origin of life, or the nature of time); rather, they dealt with specificities (what was the best design for an army barracks which took into account issues such as surveillance and health?), as well as being more closely tied up with operating and maintaining political power than the natural sciences.

Identity. The subject takes on an identity within processes of discursive designation and location: the body-as-content is designated as being commensurate, or otherwise, with regard to socio-cultural and/or scientific categories, and is thus inscribed in terms of certain meanings, values, dispositions, orientations and narratives.

Ideology. Refers to a system of ideas held by a particular group within a culture, which represents their interests, and the practices whereby such groups attempt to naturalise their ideas, meanings and values, or pass them off as universal and as common sense.

Interpellation. Refers to the process whereby power calls, addresses and categorises subjects.

Juridical sovereignty. The notion that laws that are reasonable, just, rational and self-evident are (or should be) the driving force and organising principle behind human society.

Knowledge. For Foucault, made up of perspectives, ideas, narratives, commentaries, rules, categories, laws, terms, explanations and definitions produced and valorised by disciplines, fields and institutions through the application of scientific principles. Different and new knowledge emerges from the struggle between the different areas within a culture.

Liberalism. An attitude and practice that monitors and works to limit the control, intrusion or intervention of the state in the social, economic and cultural activities of its citizens; in Foucault's terms, it is concerned with 'how not to be governed' by the state.

Micro-power. Refers to the notion that discourses 'write' the body, or shape the ways in which bodies are understood and how they function.

Modernity. Used in disciplines such as philosophy, historiography and sociology, it generally refers to that period of (western) history that dates from the Enlightenment, and that is characterised by scientific rationality, the development of commerce and capitalism, and the rise of education, surveillance, urbanism and atheism.

Neo-liberalism. The dominant economic paradigm in the western world over recent decades, characterised by the freeing up of financial markets, reduced economic regulation, and reduced or removed protective barriers such as tariffs. For Foucault, neo-liberalism constitutes a permanent critique on behalf of market forces of the limits and extent of the state and government mechanisms.

Normalisation and norms. The association of bodily exemplars and typologies with authorised meanings, narratives and values in order to discipline, dispose and orient subjects.

Normative judgements. Used to assess and monitor the actions and attitudes of people according to the notion of a norm or average. Such judgements work throughout various institutions such as prisons, schools and hospitals, as well as throughout the social body as a whole, to divide the 'normal' from the 'abnormal'.

Oedipus complex. A term taken from psychoanalysis, referring to the child's repressed desire for the mother and rivalry with the father.

Order of things. For Foucault, a combination of the institutions, forms of knowledge, discourses and practices that organise an episteme, and that make some things and activities possible and explicable and other things unthinkable. The reason for, or the logic of, such 'order' provides the foundation for social practices and systems of social organisation, without necessarily being visible itself.

Panopticism. A concept derived from Bentham's model of the panopticon, which was a tower placed in a central position within the prison. From this tower, the guards would be able to observe every cell and the prisoners inside it; however, it was designed in such a way that the prisoners would never know whether they were being observed or not. Prisoners would assume that they could be observed at any moment and would adjust their behaviour accordingly.

Parrhesia. A term that can be dated to the fifth century BC and is still found in use, having evolved in meaning across Greek and Roman culture, eight centuries later (Foucault 2001: 11). *Parrhesia* can be translated as 'free or fearless speech'. It refers both to a type of content (the parrhesiastes provides a full and candid account of the subject's thoughts and opinions on a particular matter) and a form of relationship with others. The purpose is not to use rhetorical devices to persuade, but rather to demonstrate to interlocutors that there is a corollary between one's words and one's beliefs and actions.

Pastoral power. One of the most enduring forms of power through western history, emerging in Judean practice and continuing throughout the Christian era, expressed in the image of the shepherd guiding a flock, making sure that the sheep do not stray, are kept safe from prey and are properly fed and cared for. Pastoral power was tailored to a social context in which people accepted the authority of figures in church and state as acting as benevolent guides for the journey through life and beyond.

Power. For Foucault, power is not a thing, nor is it possessed by individuals or groups. Rather, it is both a complex flow and a set of relations between different groups and areas of society that changes with circumstances and time. Another important point Foucault makes about power is that it is not solely negative (working to repress or control people)—it is also highly productive. Power produces resistance to itself. Power produces what we are and what we can do, and influences or determines how we see ourselves and the world.

Power–knowledge. Refers to Foucault's argument that forces of power are predicated upon, imbricated with and facilitated by various bodies of authorised knowledge.

Problematisation. A critical technique whereby the relation between various socio-cultural institutions, concepts, meanings, genres and practices is rethought and negotiated in a moment of crisis. A 'problematic field of experience' is a cultural space where thought and meaning temporarily have become unmoored.

Reflexivity. To think at, and through, limits that are constitutive of how we come to see, categorise, understand and relate to the world and to ourselves.

Representation. The use of greater abstraction in meaning-making: signs stand in for, but do not resemble, the object under discussion. The basis of alphabetical writing. *See also* Resemblance.

Repressive hypothesis. In *The History of Sexuality: Volume 1*, Foucault critiques the idea that power functions solely as a form of domination and repression. For example, the repressive hypothesis suggests that sexual desire was effectively repressed during certain periods, such as the Victorian Age, before giving way to 'sexual liberation'. Foucault argues instead that power actively produces and shapes all forms of conduct.

Resemblance. A way of thinking about the world through signs (words, images, gestures) that typically is associated with meaning-making up to the sixteenth century in Europe. The point is that the word, image or gesture used to stand in for the object under discussion actually and literally resembles that object. The basis of pictographic writing. *See also* Representation.

Resistance. Foucault stresses that the capacity for resistance is an integral property of power relations, first because forms of knowledge, discourses and categories are not natural but effects of power and therefore amenable to alternative understandings; and second because power is productive rather than repressive—the forms of subjectivities it produces can be performed in a resistant manner. For example, the 'delinquent' is a form of subjectivity that is resistant to disciplinary power.

Salvation. Foucault introduces the Hellenistic and Roman versions of what is understood by salvation by first separating them from what they are not. The Platonic idea of salvation is a somewhat distant relative, largely because it functions almost entirely as a philosophical rather than what Foucault refers to as a spiritual concept—and even then it lacks 'specific and strict meaning'. In Christianity, the opposite is true: salvation is strongly informed by a binary logic, always referring to some kind of movement from a fallen, abject, ignorant or corrupted state (identified with sin, death, mortality, despair, evil) to something infinitely finer and better (grace, everlasting life, certainty, goodness).

Sexuality. Libidinal regimes, orientations, dispositions and practices. In Western culture, these are often understood as constituting an identity, an understanding that Foucault argues is a product of particular discursive regimes.

Social contract theory. The notion that people freely choose to submit to the dictates and laws of the state in exchange for its protection.

Soul. For Foucault, rather than being a fundamental part of us that guides our moral life, the soul is an effect of a political anatomy.

The modern conception of the soul—which, unlike the soul born in Christian theology, is not born in sin, but includes notions of ego and psyche—is the product of practices of power and knowledge centred on the body, and is part of the wider processes of disciplinarity and biopower.

Speaking positions. The positions from which subjects are authorised to speak, and which shape the discursive practices they express, the power relations they effect and forms of knowledge upon which they draw. For example, doctors speak from a particular position of authority that authorises them to express judgements about a patient's bodily condition.

Subject. The result of a process involving the reiteration of discourses, performances and narratives of, and the repeated confirmation of relations of value regarding, the body, which make that body potentially visible and recognisable as a coherent set of forms, categories and meanings.

Subjection and subjectivity. Terms derived from psychoanalytic theory that describe and explain the process whereby the category of the human is constituted, recognised and applied to forms of life via the workings of power. These terms stand opposed to the commonsense notion of the individual as agent.

Subjugated knowledge. A form of knowledge that has been 'buried' under the official or dominant forms of knowledge that emerge within a social order.

Symbolic violence. The techniques, discourses and regimes of practice whereby the other is dehumanised or rendered abject.

Technologies. For Foucault, this refers to two main functions or mechanisms: first, the ways in which societies pacify, dominate and regulate subjects; and second, 'technologies of the self', through which subjects shape their own bodies and thoughts.

Warfare society. Refers to the idea that all social activity can be explained in terms of struggles between different sections of society. Marxism is an example of this position.

Will to power. Foucault takes this concept from Nietzsche; it refers to the notion that meanings, ideas, rules, discourses, knowledge and truths do not emerge naturally, but are produced in order to support, advantage or valorise a particular social group.

I
~
Questions of method

Introduction

This book provides a detailed and exemplified account of Foucault's methods and theories, while also showing how his work on power, discourse, subjectivity, disciplinarity, surveillance and normativity can contribute to our understanding of the contemporary world and its practices. We begin by considering Foucault's methodology as it applied to historical research, exploring how it differs in significant ways from conventional historicism. We then devote five chapters to what we consider to be the most significant theoretical issues covered by his oeuvre: the power–knowledge nexus, governance and the reason of state, liberalism and neo-liberalism, subjectivity and technologies of the self, and critique and ethics.

While Foucault traces concepts such as madness, punishment and sexuality across different historical eras, in a sense he can be identified as a historian of the present. This is because he would take a matter of concern or problematic relation from the time in which he lived and worked (such as prison reform in the 1970s in France) and then trace the historical forces that had shaped that problem. This means that the different historical periods and actors with which Foucault is concerned are, in a sense, inventions of our own time: we progressively reconstruct the past in order to serve the interests of the present. In this sense, the nineteenth century did not occur between 1801 and 1900, but rather is an ongoing invention that has been subject to revisions and reconstructions through each subsequent era. So, rather than thinking of history as a single, fixed entity, Foucault postulates multiple overlapping and contesting histories.

It is worth considering the ways in which Foucault's approach differs from other ways of making sense of history. History writing (that is, historiography) in its modern form can be dated from the early nineteenth century, when GF Hegel developed a theory of dialectics. This conceived of history in terms of the clash of opposite forces (or thesis and antithesis) that would be resolved by the development of a synthesis between these opposing forces, culminating in a higher state of human development. Karl Marx applied Hegel's dialectic theory to the material conditions of society—the distribution of economic resources. According to Marx's dialectic materialism, the clash over material economic resources between the bourgeoisie (owners of the means of production) and the proletariat (factory workers) would be resolved through revolution. This dialectic struggle would lead to a new synthesis, a communist utopia in which the fruits of labour would be distributed to all according to their needs. Curiously, the collapse of communist states in Eastern Europe in the late 1980s prompted the US writer Francis Fukuyama (1991) to talk of a new synthesis represented by the triumph of western-style democracies. The US president George Bush took up this idea when he spoke of a 'new world order' in the lead-up to the first Gulf War in 1991. And in the 2000s, the so-called war on terror and the invasions of Afghanistan (2001) and Iraq (2003) were justified in the west by characterising those actions as a defence of civilisation and democratic freedoms against the threats posed by a barbaric and 'feudal' Islam.

Foucault identifies a number of problems with dialectical and progressive views of history. First, they both tend to postulate the clash of an advanced civilised west with a backward and uncivilised rest of the world (both Hegel and Marx were supporters of colonial practice). Second, they tend to conceive of the forces of history largely in terms of the great ideological belief systems that emerged during and after the Enlightenment: liberalism, capitalism, socialism, communism and so forth. As we will discuss further in this and later chapters, Foucault is interested in how disciplinary and other forces and power relations developed alongside and within these Enlightenment discourses and ideologies. So, for example, while the ideology of liberalism preaches the values of individual freedom of expression and belief, disciplinary power was working through sites such as schools and workshops to quietly coerce people into forms of behaviour and attitudes of mind amenable to the interests of these disciplinary institutions, and the more general social practices they helped constitute.

A third problem Foucault has with the dialectical and progressive accounts of history is that they are based on a grand or totalising vision. That is, they suggest that we can fit the various events that take place over time into a pattern, according to certain laws of historical development. Against this synthetic view of history (the idea that different events can be synthesised to form a coherent whole), Foucault conceives of history in terms of plurality—a multiple number of events that are as often as much in conflict with one another as they can be held together. For Foucault, history is conceived of in terms of discontinuity and disjuncture as well as continuity and conjuncture. Rather than seeing historical time unfolding in an orderly, continuous, linear manner in which various historical events can be conjoined or fitted together to form regular patterns, Foucault thinks of history as an ongoing struggle between different forces and forms of power. His historical research reconstructs the conditions for the appearance of a phenomenon—such as the birth of the prison—on the basis of multiple determining elements, from which it arises as an effect.

Foucault argues that not only is there disjuncture and discontinuity between different historical events, there is also a disjuncture and discontinuity between historians and the historical events they seek to describe. The historian and history speak from different places. The historian speaks from an authorised position within a public institution such as a museum, archive or university. The historian may engage in fieldwork and archival search, but it is the protocols and procedures of the institution that will shape how the history will be written, and how the different historical events will be fitted together to form a coherent vision. This process covers over certain gaps in the record—the historical material that has been lost or has not been collected. The oral histories of indigenous peoples and the folk tales of peasants find no place within the written historical records, but they continue to assert a presence through their absence, thus potentially opening up gaps within the historiographical enterprise.

In challenging the authority of the historian, Foucault draws attention to another problem with conventional historiography—the presumption that it begins with the unified subject. This view of history is that historical events occurred as a consequence of the various motivations of different historical actors. Accordingly, it is the duty of historiography to work through these motivations and recreate the thought patterns and sensibilities of significant historical figures. This approach belongs to the 'great men of history' school that focuses on the lives of powerful and successful monarchs, explorers, generals and politicians, such as Queen Elizabeth I, Christopher Columbus, Napoleon and Adolf Hitler. For Foucault, this approach misses the point that subjects, actions and meanings are shaped by the discursive and non-discursive forces that flow through the positions occupied by these figures. What discourses was Hitler drawing on or speaking through in order to be able to depict Jewish people not as human beings but as entirely different forms of life? What disciplinary forces and movements shaped his bodily actions during the Nuremberg rallies, such that they had a profound impact on the behaviours and attitudes of others? Indeed, the 'founding subject' or 'great men' conception of history is complicit with liberal humanist discourses and ideologies that emerged from the European Enlightenment; these were associated with Cartesian philosophy, which asserts that human reason and rationality are germane to historical change.

A further problem associated with such a conception of history is that it silences whole categories of people. Women, as well as indigenous and colonised peoples, have traditionally been marginalised within such historiography. As Michel de Certeau points out (1988), this kind of historiography is complicit with the practices of colonialism. It divides people into subjects and objects, active and passive; on the one hand there are the colonising people who make history and develop forms of knowledge, and on the other the colonised people who are made the object of such history and knowledge.

We can articulate Foucault's understanding of historical forces (including the construction of historical knowledge) with his interest in power relations. He developed this concern with practices of power through the research methods he called archaeology and genealogy (which we discuss in detail later in this and subsequent chapters). Basically, both methods work to uncover the discursive formations and practices of different historical periods; however, genealogy has a greater focus on the ways in which discursive power works on bodies. Power shows itself on a subject's body because various events or happenings are 'written' on the body—they shape the ways in which we perform, or act out, our bodily selves.

Beyond historicism

At the beginning of the Collège de France lecture series published in *The Birth of Biopolitics* (2008), Foucault is talking about the content of the course, which is intended to both retrace and continue on from the previous year's series on the art of government (Foucault 2007a). After a few introductory remarks, he raises the issue of methodology, and quickly and explicitly differentiates his method from those forms of sociological, historical and political analysis that presume 'real government practices' originate from, and are articulated through and by, 'already given objects' (2008: 2)—by which he means concepts-as-phenomena such as the state, the people and civil society. Foucault proposes to do:

> exactly the opposite . . . I would like to start with . . . concrete practices and . . . pass these universals through the grid of these practices . . . I start from the theoretical and methodological decision that consists in saying . . . How can you write history if you do not accept *a priori* the existence of things like the state, society, the sovereign, and subjects . . . So what I would like to deploy here is exactly the opposite of historicism: not, then, questioning universals by using history as a critical method, but starting from the decision that universals do not exist, asking what kind of history we can do (2008: 2–3).

In these two sets of lectures (2007a, 2008), Foucault provides a genealogy of the processes and mechanisms whereby particular forms, logics, programs and values of governance are universalised, and effectively placed outside history. By way of example, Foucault argues that it is not the state that gives rise to the set of procedures, imperatives, institutions, categories, discourses and practices that developed in the sixteenth and seventeeth centuries as the reason of state. On the contrary, for Foucault the reason of state 'is precisely a practice, or rather the rationalisation of a practice, which places itself between a state presented as a given and a state presented as having to be constructed and built' (2008: 4). In other words, the interests of the amalgam of forces and procedures that constitute the reason of state require a particular kind of state, for two related reasons. First, the state as an *a priori* point of origin authorises and guarantees the validity of the reason of state. Second, the idea of the state as something that is an end in itself, but that also requires constant renewal, reinforcement and maintenance, legitimises and facilitates the activities and logics of the reason of state. This includes the transformation of people into a population, the extension of disciplinary and normative mechanisms, and various interventions in areas such as health, education, crime and punishment, architecture, town planning, commerce, transport, the family and the military.

Foucault attempts to explain and negotiate the amalgam and interrelation of forces, discourses, institutions, fields, technologies, actions and contexts that work to produce and naturalise things-as-sense—the state, the world as historically explicable narrative—via the notion of the apparatus, or *dispositif*. Giorgio Agamben refers to an apparatus as:

> literally anything that has in some way the capacity to capture, orient, determine, intercept, model, control, or secure the gestures, behaviors, opinions, or discourses of living beings. Not only, therefore, prisons, madhouses, the panopticon, schools, confessions, factories, disciplines, judicial measures, and so forth (whose connection with power is in a certain sense evident), but also the pen, writing, literature, philosophy, agriculture, cigarettes, navigation, computers, cellular phones and . . . language itself, which is perhaps the most ancient of apparatuses (Agamben 2009: 14).

The relation between these elements, and the significances, dispositions, orientations and activities that are consequences of them, can be understood as a relation between power and its effects, but with an important and radical intervention on Foucault's part. Power for Foucault is not a possession (the king holds power), the result of a primary cause (God bestows power) or a thing in itself (power selects those who would best carry out its designs). Nor is it something that is willed, in the Nietzschean sense. Rather, power is always relational, and the rhythms and flows of power are both arbitrary (in the sense that any configuration of ideas, technologies and contexts is an accident, subject to the dislocations of time and place) and motivated (what is naturalised as powerful always seeks to arrest that situation, for its own benefit).

Genealogy is one of the two main forms of methodology—the other being archaeology—utilised by Foucault in an attempt to identify the traces, trajectories and flows of power; we will deal with these in some detail later in this chapter. Both methodologies can be characterised as constituting a reaction to, a rejection of and an attempt to move beyond conventional historicism, to which Foucault attributes two main problematical tendencies. The first of these, to do with the question of origins, has already been touched on, but it requires some elaboration. The notion of a point of origin from which all other events, ideas and categories are derived has always played a significant role in history and historiography, although this function has differed from one period to another. Foucault refers, for instance, to those histories written in the Middle Ages that 'spoke of the antiquity of kingdoms, brought great ancestors back to life, and rediscovered the heroes who founded empires and dynasties' (2003b: 66). So the establishment of a line of continuity linking a kingdom to a fabled place and time of origin (say, involving Rome, or even further back to Troy) meant that the glories of the past (royal families, legendary battles, journeys and other events) worked to 'guarantee the value of the present, and transform its pettiness and mundanity into something equally heroic and equally legitimate' (2003b: 66). Foucault contrasts this with modern history and its search for, and discovery of, the founding moment that gives rise to yet escapes history. This is a historicity that:

> in its very fabric, makes possible the necessity of an origin which must both be internal and foreign to it: like the virtual tip of a cone in which all differences, all dispersions, all discontinuities would be knitted together so as to form no more than

a single point of identity, the impalpable figure of the Same (1973: 329–30).

The examples Foucault has in mind here are 'the two types of historical interpretation developed in the nineteenth century' (2003b: 272): one is class struggle, the other race and biological determinism. The former is associated with the Marxist account of history. Marxism appropriates Hegel's mechanism of the dialectic in order to set in train a narrative of history—the triumph of the proletariat—that effectively abolishes history. With the latter, a theme of state racism finds its origin in a 'mythological landscape' (popularised by Wagner, among others) of primordial struggles and warriors who galvanise and guide the people—a theme that is taken up and developed most prominently by the Nazis. We have already referred to Fukuyama's (1992) reference to a Hegelian-inflected liberal-capitalist 'end of history', where market-driven liberal democracy has settled all the big questions, vanquished ideological competitors and brought into being a history without history, or a history punctuated by variations on the universal that is democratic capitalism.

The second historicising tendency against which Foucault reacts is the representation of history as continuity. Foucault identifies tradition as one of the concepts that performs this kind of function; it is here understood as both a narrative and bureaucratic mechanism that makes it 'possible to register all innovations with respect to a system of permanent coordinates and to give a status to an ensemble of constant phenomena' (1998: 302). If we were to consider the field of literary studies in the nineteenth and twentieth centuries, for example, we could see in the work of prominent and influential critics such as Mathew Arnold, Eric Auerbach, Ernst Curtius and TS Eliot the identification or presumption of a cultural tradition running from Greek and Roman antiquity, through the Middle Ages and the Renaissance, to the present. This tradition-as-history is a kind of grid of intelligibility through and against which all cultural texts and practitioners, and all movements, trends and genres, are measured. This tradition recognises, organises, allocates value, differentiates, and arranges hierarchies and affiliations; in short, it produces an unhistorical account of historical monumentalities (Shakespeare, Milton, Romanticism). Manifestations of apparent difference or discontinuity are registered as strange dead ends, superficial or limited by their provincial attachment to time and place—although the question of whether a body of work is universal or particular can be the source of considerable struggle or even internecine warfare (consider the history of critical debates within English departments regarding the value of DH Lawrence's oeuvre).

This work of canonisation and exclusion is effected and normalised across authorised pedagogical, cultural and social institutions and sites, such as schools, galleries, museums and universities—and, perhaps more contemporaneously, within the electronic media. The humanities faculties of western universities, for instance, have universalised the 'edifice of humanistic knowledge resting on the classics of European letters' (Said 1984: 21), to the exclusion of other non-European traditions, and without regard to or recognition of the particular politics (of class, race and gender) that fashion this image of the universal. As Edward Said writes:

When our students are taught such things as 'the humanities', they are almost always taught that these classic texts embody, express, represent what is best in our, that is, the only, tradition. Moreover they are taught that such fields as the humanities . . . exist in a relatively neutral political element, that they are to be appreciated and venerated, that they define the limits of what is acceptable, appropriate, and legitimate so far as culture is concerned. In other words, the affiliate order so presented surreptitiously duplicates the closed and tightly knit familial structure that secures generational hierarchical relationships to one another. Affiliation then becomes in effect a literal form of re-presentation, by which what is ours is good . . . and what is not ours in this ultimately provincial sense is simply left out (1984: 21–2).

Tradition is one of the forms of authorisation that work to organise and normalise history as a vertical continuity. This narrative function is also extended and flattened out at a horizontal level, via categories and designations such as genre, field, discipline, authorship, oeuvre, mentality, movement and school. As Foucault (1998) points out, these vertical and horizontal groupings, no matter how apparently intuitive or material-based, are always implicated in and derived from networks and forces of power. To paraphrase Nietzsche, we can say that such categories, collections and unities are the manifestations of power as practice. Even the most taken-for-granted, everyday designation, such as the book:

> is not a homogenous unity: the relations that exist between different mathematical treatises are not the same as those existing between different philosophical texts. The difference between one of Stendhal's novels cannot be superimposed upon that which separates two volumes of the Human Comedy . . . Further, the edges of a book are neither clear nor rigorously delineated. No book exists by itself, it is always in a relation of support and dependence *vis-à-vis* other books . . . However much the book is given as an object one might have in hand . . . its unity is variable and relative (1998: 304).

The Order of Things

If history is characterised by discontinuity as much as it is by unity and repetition, there remains the problem of how and why the various social, cultural and political narratives and accounts of unity and continuity do their work. Put simply, how do bodies of knowledge—and, by extension, forces of power—synthesise and normalise the disparate, the contrary, the arbitrary and the heterogeneous—and to what purpose and effects? This set of questions serves as an entry point for a wider consideration of Foucault's methodological trajectories: for instance, it informs the study of the relation between epistemic continuity and discontinuity in *Madness and Civilization*; the structuralist-inflected scholarship of *The Order of Things* and *The Birth of the Clinic*; the analysis of the notions and functions of discourse and discursive regimes in *The Archaeology of Knowledge*; the genealogical inquiries into normative and disciplinary apparatuses and work, and the development of biopower, in *Discipline and Punish* and the first volume of *The History of Sexuality*; and the tracing of the gradual transformation of the practices and political functions of history and historiography in the Collège de France lectures that are reproduced and collected in *Society Must Be Defended*.

Foucault begins the Preface to *The Order of Things* (1973) with an admission that this book:

first arose out of a passage in Borges, out of the laughter that shattered, as I read the passage, all the familiar landscapes of my thought—*our* thought, the thought that bears the stamp of our age and our geography—breaking up all the ordered surfaces and all the planes with which we are accustomed to tame the wild profusion of existing things . . . This passage quotes a 'certain Chinese encyclopaedia' in which it is written that 'animals are divided into: (a) belonging to the Emperor, (b) embalmed, (c) tame, (d) sucking pigs, (e) sirens, (f) fabulous, (g) stray dogs, (h) included in the present classification, (i) frenzied, (j) innumerable, (k) drawn with a very fine camelhair brush, (l) et cetera, (m) having just broken the water pitcher, (n) that from a long way off look like flies'. In the wonderment of this taxonomy, the thing we apprehend in one great leap . . .

is demonstrated as the exotic charm of another system of thought, is the limitation of our own, the stark impossibility of thinking *that* (1973: xv).

This (fictional) classificatory system is not just exotic—it is in no sense congruent with our familiar, everyday world-view. One of the more obvious points of difference is the basis, logic or rationale on which the system is ordered: we can say, for instance, that in contradistinction to contemporary western thought, there is an unproblematic articulation between the socio-political regime and forms of knowledge, since the position and status of the emperor is clearly one of its organising principles; and that the categories (sirens, fabulous, etc.) contained here indicate that those forms of knowledge are incommensurable with western science.

Equally disconcerting, interesting and useful to Foucault is the heterotopic nature of this classificatory system. As he points out, utopian historical narratives usually are characterised by neatness and certainty, an easy and clear articulation from one point of reference to another, and a sense of arrangement that allows space to unfold in an ordered manner (1973: xviii). Heterotopias, on the other hand, 'desiccate speech, stop words in their track' and 'dissolve our myths' (1973: xviii). The example he uses here is well known to structuralist linguistics: it is that of the aphasiac, who finds it difficult to arrange or order things in terms of conventional notions of likeness or similarity (based on a single category such as colour or shape), but 'will create a multiplicity of tiny, fragmented regions in which nameless resemblances agglutinate things into unconnected islets' (1973: xviii). So, instead of arranging all the yellow objects with the yellow and the red with the red, the aphasiac will collect things together based on a system of categorisation that is, or appears to be, internally incommensurable (colour, tactile quality, length, shape). Moreover, this aphasiac heterotopia is always a temporary arrangement: the 'sick mind continues to infinity, creating groups then dispersing them again, heaping up diverse similarities, destroying those that seem clearest, splitting up things that are identical' (1973: xviii).

Borges' taxonomy, like the arrangements of aphasics, is a structure that can't function in any conventional sense, yet it is represented as being a product of the culture of China, whose 'name alone constitutes for the west a vast reservoir of utopias . . . In our traditional imagery, the Chinese culture is the most meticulous, the most rigidly ordered, the one . . . most attached to the pure delineation of space' (1973: xix). Borges' Chinese anti-taxonomy draws our attention to the possibility of another China—albeit a fictional one—that is somehow incommensurate, foreign and unfamiliar with regard to the China that is found in popular western culture (the China of historical romances, Hollywood epics and television travel programs).

For Foucault, the Borges example and the work it performs served as a departure point for three theoretical considerations that would inform not just the quasi-structuralism of *The Order of Things*, but all his subsequent archaeological and genealogical work. First, what are the grounds on which a system of classification can be founded—or, in other words, 'What is this coherence . . . which . . . is neither determined by an *a priori* . . . nor imposed upon us by immediately perceptible contents?' (1973: xix). Things are not given to us in an unmediated form (for example, the life forms in the Linnaean system have existed for millions of years, but they have only come to be understood in relation to other life forms-as-categories since the eighteenth century), nor do they remain the same (that system of identification and resemblance has been superseded/modified by Darwin's theory of evolution, and the Darwinian system has itself been modified extensively in the twentieth century).

Second, what is the extent and character of the operation of ordering things? The example Foucault gives is this: when we state that there is greater familial resemblance between two dogs than, say, between a dog and a cat, the intuitive dimension to this move—the ground on which we are able to recognise and normalise motivated arbitrariness as reality—is the result of a great deal of work. Rather than simply observing an objectivity, in this act we are subjecting a 'proliferation of qualities and forms' (1973: xix–xx) to all encompassing scrutiny, analysis, comparison, measurement, description and differentiation:

> there is no similitude and no distinction, even for the wholly untrained perception, that is not the result of a precise operation and of the application of a preliminary criterion. A 'system of elements'—a definition of the segments by which the resemblances and differences can be shown, the types of variation by which these segments can be affected, and, lastly, the threshold above which there is difference and below which there is similitude—is indispensable for the establishment of even the simplest form of order (1973: xx).

To relate this point to our Linnaean examples, we simply need to do a Google search using the expression 'history of mammals as classificatory category', and click on the Wikipedia entry for 'mammal' (<http://en.wikipedia.org/wiki/Mammal>). What we find is less a history of a classificatory system than a normalised retroactivity. References to and descriptions of characteristics, lines of descent and infraclass taxa dating from the eighteenth century onwards are deployed as if they were both out of time and non-methodological; they function as a form of unmediated truth that allows us to see and understand life forms, and relations between them, dating from the Jurassic period almost 200 million years ago. What is in fact a historically based system of thought is represented and read as an unmediated (scientific) reality. Pierre Bourdieu (1991) uses the term 'social magic' to describe processes of this kind. A certain materiality (institutions, books, lists, experiments, data), authorised and legitimated by a field possessing considerable cultural capital (biological science), transcends itself to the extent that it takes on a mystical quality and performs the work of producing immediate and intuitive belief and acceptance on the part of its audiences—and not just other scientists, but across the wider socio-cultural field. At some point, this magic leaves one authority (a book, a system, a name, a school) and inhabits another (Newton is superseded by Einstein) without the credibility or legitimacy of the new relationship being impugned or called into question by what has gone before.

This leads us to the third theoretical issue, which we can refer to as the relation between historical continuity and discontinuity. We will quote Foucault's description of this relation-as-process at length here:

> The fundamental codes of a culture . . . establish for every man, from the very first, the empirical orders with which he will be dealing and within which he will be at home. At the other extremity of thought, there are the scientific theories . . . which explain why order exists in general, what universal laws to obey . . . and why this particular order has been established and not some other. But between these two regions, so distant from one another, lies a domain which, even though its role is mainly an intermediary one, is nonetheless fundamental . . . It is here that a culture, imperceptibly deviating from the empirical orders prescribed by its primary codes, instituting an initial separation from them, causes them to lose their original transparency, relinquishes its immediate and invisible power, frees itself sufficiently to discover that these orders are perhaps not the only possible ones or the best ones . . . Thus between the already 'encoded' eye and reflexive knowledge there is a middle region which liberates order itself . . . Thus, in every culture . . . there is the pure experience of order and of its modes of being. The present study is an attempt to analyse this experience (1973: xx–xxi).

In *The Order of Things*, Foucault addresses these issues in a particularly detailed manner. The first point he makes is that contemporary western culture is derived from the playing out of this relation between three epistemological paradigms: reflexive knowledge (produced by and through authorised fields, particularly the human sciences), the logics of everyday practice, and that in-between region where what was once straightforward, obvious, intuitive and supposedly natural becomes problematic. The transition from one paradigm to another is formulated at the level of an abstraction (reflexivity produces falsification, and falsification produces paradigm shifts), and remains within the logics of progress and positivism (reflexivity and falsification work to lay bare the world, to reveal its laws, and to provide improved and potentially perfected knowledge). However, Foucault's work is concerned not with determining which paradigms are closer to reality or constitute the truth, but with forming an understanding of how certain paradigms come to stand for and function as truth.

Archaeology and the episteme

The distinction Foucault posits is between a history of ideas (which would include and remain constant to the universalism of science-as-progress) and a form of inquiry that aims to:

> rediscover on what basis knowledge and theory became possible; within what space of order knowledge was constituted; on the basis of what historical *a priori* . . . ideas could appear, sciences be established . . . rationalities be formed, only, perhaps, to dissolve and vanish soon afterwards . . . Such an enterprise is not so much a history, in the traditional meaning of that word, as an 'archaeology' (1973: xxii).

One of the functions of archaeological inquiry is to reveal the discontinuities at the heart of western culture—discontinuities that are constitutive of the fiction of western culture as linear, universal, progressive and continuous. This inquiry simultaneously involves and presumes another kind of inquiry: it is predicated on the provision of an account and analysis of a totality of relations that produce continuity and sameness. This totality of relations is what Foucault refers to as an episteme, and it extends across different ages and their various fields and disciplines, including those that have disappeared or lost their legitimacy.

What does Foucault understand by the term 'episteme'? An episteme provides the logics, narratives and dispositions through which subjects see, understand and relate to the world. It constitutes:

> the strategic apparatus which permits of separating out from among all the statements which are possible those that will be acceptable within, I won't say a scientific theory, but a field of scientificity, and which it is possible to say are true or false. The episteme is the 'apparatus' which makes possible the separation, not of the true from the false, but of what may from what may not be characterised as scientific (Foucault 1980: 197).

Epistemes organise, categorise and evaluate the discursive and material phenomena of a time/place, in the process producing some ideas, values and narratives as natural, doxic, normal or universal, and others as unthinkable. As de Certeau writes:

> Between the many institutions, experiences, and doctrines of an age, he [Foucault] detects a coherence which, though not explicit, is nonetheless the condition and organizing principle of a culture. There is, therefore, order. But this 'Reason' is a ground that escapes the notice of the very people whose ideas and exchanges it provides the foundation for. No one can express in words that which gives everyone the power to speak. There is order, but only in the form of what one does not know (de Certeau 1984: 172).

An example offered by Foucault is of the Renaissance naturalist Ulisse Aldrovandi. Aldrovandi was a professor of natural philosophy at the University of Bologna, and a highly regarded naturalist. As a philosopher/scientist, he was someone both trained and practiced in observation, and in careful analysis; his taxonomy of the natural world had great traction for a time. He was also an expert in draconology (the study of dragons). In 1572 he took possession of a dragon that had been menacing the countryside around Bologna, studied it and displayed it to visitors in his private museum. Subsequently he wrote a history of the dragon, *Dracologia* (published posthumously), which incorporated research information about dragons, including their history and their physiology. His attention to the world of legend was not limited to dragons: in scientific works such as his *Monstrorum historia* (1642), he made no distinctions between natural and mythological creatures—each had its place in his system of classification. By the eighteenth century, his work had been discounted by most naturalists, mainly because of its tendency to mix science with fantasy. Georges-Louis Leclerc, the Comte de Buffon, wrote scathingly of his contribution to knowledge because of this fantastical element, but Foucault takes a different perspective. He writes that Aldrovandi:

> was neither a better nor a worse observer than Buffon; he was neither more credulous than he, nor less attached to the faithfulness of the observing eye or to the rationality of things. His observation was simply not linked to things in accordance with the same arrangement of the episteme (1973: 40).

Aldrovandi operated careful and reliable scientific techniques in perfect accordance with what constituted science in his age—the concept that all that exists is there to be read. What this demonstrates is that even the act of seeing—a natural faculty—is culturally framed: dragons have not been seen in Europe, or at least not by scientists, since the classical era (the eighteenth century). For us they are unseeable,

19

but for Aldrovandi they were not only visible, but knowable. His work counted as good science in its time; by the 1700s, however, it would be seen as flawed.

For Foucault, knowledge/episteme is what makes it possible to name one thing as true and another as false—not on the basis of any final proof, but rather on the basis of how facts, ideas, evidence and the wide world are currently understood. In different epistemes, the status of truth can be given to, and taken from, the same methodologies, discourses, beliefs and narratives. For instance, in the fifteenth century, articles of faith and church dogmas were held to be entirely true in principle. While the Reformation showed the cracks in the logic, nonetheless it is fair to say that virtually everyone thought in terms of a world governed finally by a divine entity. It would have been virtually unthinkable for people living in that period to perceive the world as the product of random forces, or social mores as the result of individual ethical choices.

In Foucault's work, what becomes evident is that while the change from one episteme to another is always a point of rupture, a radical break from one way of seeing and knowing to another, that change is not necessarily evident to those who live in one episteme, or through the break. There are always continuities along with the discontinuities; this is especially true with everyday practices, subjected as they are to the conservative disposition of the habitus. As Foucault writes, 'within the space of a few years a culture sometimes ceases to think as it had been thinking up till then and begins to think other things in a new way'; and change 'probably begins with an erosion from outside' (1973: 50). De Certeau offers the following useful characterisation and exemplification of this position:

> On one level, we have a surface permanence which, despite shiftings of ground, keeps words, concepts, or symbolic themes the same. A simple example: the 'madman' is spoken of in the 16th, 17th and 19th centuries, but actually 'it is not

a question of the same malady' in any two of them. The same thing applies to theological exegesis as it does to medicine. The same words do not designate the same things. Ideas, themes, classifications float from one mental universe to another, but at each passage they are affected by structures which reorganize them and endow them with a new meaning. The same mental objects 'function' differently (1984: 179).

This 'surface permanence' is the continuity of terms and points of reference, but their denotation—or what the words actually mean in a particular period—indicates the extent of discontinuity across epistemes. De Certeau, following Foucault, points to shifts in understanding of, and practices with respect to, 'the madman' over the Renaissance and the Classical epistemes—shifts that Foucault traced in a number of works (1975, 1982, 1988a, 2006b). During the Middle Ages, for instance, madness was perceived as ambiguity and dizzying unreason (1988a: 11), and just as lepers had been excluded from society up to that point, the possible contagion of insanity was dealt with by exclusion. From the sixteenth century, madness was understood as 'present everywhere and mingled with every experience' (1988a: 66), and as the effect of coming too close to the Reason of God; as a result, those identified as mad were no longer excluded, but were allowed to live among the rest of the population. With the rise of the hegemony of the discourse of reason in the eighteenth century, the mad were still perceived as those who were unreasonable, but now this unreason was associated with animality, with shame (1988a: 64) and with the lack of a capacity to participate in society. In the nineteenth century, the focus was still on unreason, but the medicalisation of discourse meant that madness became associated with ill-health and could be investigated, known and corrected. Finally, in the contemporary period the focus has shifted to scientific research and clinical intervention. What this means is that what is now identified and understood as madness is only explicable—only comes into being, really—within a very specific set of cultural frames, discourses and ways of seeing. Perhaps even more importantly, this cultural world-view also prescribes and sets in motion both the narratives within which madness will be located (a genetic weakness that needs to be dealt with chemically, a traumatic experience that requires therapy), and the forms through which the subject-of-madness will relate to the self and to power (my madness is inherited, and bears no relation to my socio-cultural trajectory; my madness requires that I adjust to socio-cultural norms). Across recent western history, those classified as insane have been associated with a lack of reason, as well as with a form of maladjustment to society; however, what that has meant, and how the mad have been treated, has changed radically.

The western episteme

In *The Order of Things*, Foucault provides an archaeological account of three periods and forms—the Renaissance, the Classical Age and the Modern Age—that he posits as characterising the wider western episteme over the last four centuries. He refers only briefly and in passing to the first of these, the Renaissance, preferring to concentrate on the Classical Age, presumably insofar as it presages and inflects the third episteme, that of the Modern Age. There are a number of features and figures that Foucault identifies with the Classical Age, but by far the most significant is the general, over-arching narrative that the world is God's book. What this means is that there is really no question of the production of meaning, order, taxonomies or tables, because those aspects are already given in, and immanent with regard to, the world. It is God's world, and any sense that it has is derived from and given to us by the Almighty. The production of meaning is man's work, and as Foucault notes, 'Before the end of the eighteenth century, man did not exist . . . he is a quite recent creature, which the demiurge of knowledge fabricated with its own hand less than two hundred years ago' (1973: 308).

The meanings and the order of things of God's world are to be found not through the intervention or facility of human knowledge, but via the application of a method of differentiation-as-identification. This order of things can be identified, initially, at the lowest level of nature: comparisons between basic elements give rise to a 'serial arrangement which . . . will show up differences as degrees of complexity' (1973: 54). Resemblance and similitude, which in the Renaissance were the predominant basis of knowledge, are now dismissed as 'the occasion of error, the danger to which one exposes oneself when one does not examine the obscure region of confusions' (1973: 51).

Foucault quotes and refers to the works of representative intellectual and scientific figures of the Classical Age (Bacon, Descartes, Condorcet, Berkeley, Condillac, Leibnitz) in order to demonstrate the various but related forms taken by this critique. The Classical Age can generally be characterised by its rigour of observation, coupled with an empirical sensibility that supersedes the Renaissance thought, exemplified by the fictional figure of Don Quixote. Quixote lives by the books of romance, magic and chivalry, but at every turn his reliance on their textual prescriptions, accounts and advice—their maps of the world—proves to be disastrous. He resembles nothing but the figures from his books and, as Foucault points out, this produces alienation and madness rather than recognition. The facility and power of magical knowledge is of no use in a disenchanted world that stubbornly refuses to comply with or correspond to loose logic and extravagant words. It will be superseded by a predominantly mathematical model of knowledge that will tabulate and order things, rather than hermeneutically interpret the secrets of life.

The epistemic leap that allows for this more rigorous apprehension of things is partly derived, then, from a method of the differentiation and 'mathematization of the living' (1998: 264); however, as Foucault points out, for the Classical Age there also 'existed a very important domain that included general grammar, natural history and the analysis of wealth' (1998: 264). The ordering of things was informed not just by mathematics and geometry, but also by a 'systematics of signs, a sort of general and systematic taxonomy of things' (1998: 264). Whereas for Quixote and the Renaissance signs are without content, or at least are shown to be based on a model of resemblances that is unsustainable (the windmill is a giant, flocks of animals are armies, Quixote is a knight and Sancho Panza his page), in the Classical Age they take on three very different properties and characteristics: they must be relatively constant; they may apply to the whole or part of a thing they denote; and they may be both natural or conventional (1973: 58). What is involved in these three developments is, first, the replacement of the notion of the sign as a thing in itself (a natural element, and a keeper of secrets) with the idea of a network of signs, built around and through the work and authority of empirical knowledge and judgements, which will be predictive and reliable; as Foucault writes, 'the relation will be that of sign to signified . . . a relation which . . . will progress from the weakest probability towards the greatest certainty' (1973: 60). Second, and by way of extension, this system of signs, derived from and constituted through evaluation and analysis, is itself available as a means of furthering the work of analysis and judgement; it is 'the sign that enables things to become distinct . . . to dissociate themselves or bind themselves together' (1973: 61). Third, signs now perform the work of linking the arbitrary and artificial to the natural and the divine: an artificial and/but rigorous system of signs should be a 'simple, absolutely transparent language . . . capable of naming what is elementary; it is also the complex of operations which defines all possible conjunctions' (1973: 62).

This relation between the arbitrary and the natural is further developed and clarified in terms of the articulation—and forms of non-articulation—posited between the human and the natural world. Foucault argues that in the Classical Age the human is a function or mechanism that makes the order of the world apparent; and the sign is that place where 'nature and human nature intersect' (Dreyfus and Rabinow 1986: 20). What the human does not do, however, is produce signification (the meaning of nature, say); this is brought about via the intermediary of the sign constituted from knowledge. This is what Foucault is referring to when he writes that 'this universal extension of the sign . . . precludes even the possibility of a theory of signification' (1973: 65). This is because, for the Classical Age, man:

> as a primary reality with its own density, as the . . . object and sovereign subject of all possible knowledge, has no place in it. The modern themes of an individual who lives, speaks, and works in accordance with the laws of an economics, a philology, and a biology, but who also . . . has acquired the right, through the interplay of these very laws, to know them and to subject them to total clarification—all these themes so familiar to us today and linked to the existence of the 'human sciences' are excluded by Classical thought (1973: 310).

The situation is demonstrated in *The Order of Things* by a detailed analysis of the arrangement of space and subjects in Velázquez's seventeenth-century painting *Las Meninas*. Foucault refers to the ways in which the various figures and content (Velázquez, the reflection of the king and queen in a mirror, the Infanta and her companions, an unidentified observer, the canvas, light entering the room) appear as balanced and ordered elements; this is an effect that is quite deliberately, carefully and comprehensively undone in Picasso's numerous Cubist versions of *Las Meninas*, painted some three centuries later.

In Velázquez's painting, every gaze is part of a series of articulations and exchanges, and space is represented as a form of dispersal that returns within an integrated narrative. These forms of exchange and integration are brought to light via the illumination-as-Enlightenment that floods the room and 'envelopes the figures and the spectators and carries them with it, under the painter's gaze, towards the place where his brush will represent them' (1973: 6). As Foucault observes, however:

> in the midst of this dispersion which is simultaneously grouping together and spreading out before us, indicated compellingly from every side, is an essential void: the necessary disappearance of that which is its foundation . . . This very subject . . . has been elided (1973: 16).

The emergence of man into this scene of representation coincides with, and is consequent on, a 'profound upheaval' (1973: 312). The Classical episteme, and the relative transparency of the order of things, gives way to modernity, the human sciences, and man 'in his ambiguous position as an object of knowledge and as a subject that knows' (1973: 312). From this time on, 'the entire space of . . . representation' will be 'related to one corporeal gaze' and what Foucault terms 'The Analytic of Finitude' (1973: 312). This change is reflected in the transformation of disciplines of knowledge, which are now oriented towards an inquiry into things as they pertain to, inform or constitute part of the affairs of men. One example of this shift can be plotted in the movement from nature to natural history, and on to biology: the 'blind similitude of things' (1973: 160) gives way to the progression of living creatures determined in advance by God; this is in turn replaced by the theory of evolution, where man once again has the ambiguous role of being merely and simultaneously part (albeit an exceptional one) of the series that is life, and 'the source of order for the totality they form' (1973: 313).

The production of man as the principle of life is derived, Foucault argues, from a reconfiguration of the relation between things, the human, metaphysics and epistemology—what he characterises as a 'discovery of finitude' (1973: 314). Without any divine light to help illuminate order or meaning, man is left to his own devices, split between the status of a thing within things, and a more privileged but alienated role as one who is capable of and consigned to the labour of reaching an understanding of those things. In other words, the removal of God from the domain of epistemology is both a loss and an opportunity. Man's analytical work:

unveils himself to his own eyes in the form of a being who is already . . . an instrument of production, a vehicle for words which exist before him. All these contents that his knowledge reveals to him as exterior to himself, and older than his own birth . . . transverse him as though he were merely an object of nature, a face doomed to be erased in the course of history. Man's finitude is heralded . . . in the positivity of knowledge (1973: 313).

At the same time, 'man is designated—more, required—by them, since it is he who speaks, since . . . even though he is not conceived as the end-product of evolution, he is recognised to be one extremity of a long series' (1973: 313).

How does the condition of finitude function as limitation and privilege—in other words, how does it (simultaneously) interrupt and facilitate access to knowledge and truth, and what is to be the foundation of an epistemology that is authorised by nothing but itself? Foucault's answer is that it occurs by way of 'a certain thought of the Same—in which Difference is the same thing as identity' (1973: 315). This is played out in three movements where 'we shall see in succession the transcendental repeat the empirical, the cogito repeat the unthought, the return of the origin repeat its retreat' (1973: 316).

Although they occupy strongly antithetical positions within the human sciences, Comte and Marx serve as the representative figures of the forms of analysis that characterise the first movement. For Comte and the positivists, man (and, by extension, all knowledge) comes into being via an analysis of the various ways in which the human body perceives and registers phenomena—or, as Foucault expresses it, 'there is a nature of human knowledge that determines its forms and that at the same time be made manifest to it in its own empirical contents' (1973: 319). The body is, from this perspective, a privileged site in the sense that it registers, observes and analyses, and also produces accounts of, the laws of nature. We can see how this demonstrates

Foucault's formulation of the transcendent repeating the empirical: the truth of the body gives rise to a technical discourse that, although different to experience, becomes one and the same with that experience (this formulation eventually degenerates across the human sciences into a naïve empiricism). With Marx, the processes run in the opposite direction; however, they retain the same fundamental logic: the transcendent given of history (class struggle) provides the grounds for the recuperation of the diversity of experience into the Same. The truth of actual experience is revealed through the mechanism of history that makes analysis, and by extension the apprehension of the truth of history, possible.

The second and third movements, involving the relation between consciousness (and what remains outside or beyond it) and the issue of the return of origins, 'form an overlapping series' (Dreyfus and Rabinow 1986: 41) with the first, again tied to the question of epistemology. The representative modern theorist of otherness and the unconscious is Freud, who discovers that the truth of man is what is not and cannot be known, and holds out the promise of a modification-through-intervention of that condition. This bridging of the gap that separates consciousness and its other will be accomplished via the methods of psychoanalysis.

With the issue of origins, the emphasis on or question of finitude, as Foucault explains it, passes from 'the weight of things upon man' and his domination 'by life, history, and language' to 'the insurmountable relation of man's being with time' (1973: 335). For philosophers such as Nietzsche and Heidegger, the idea of a point of origin that explicates and drives human history, as posited by Hegel and Marx, is countered by the notion of an eternal return (the will to power), or an intuition of what has receded (authentic being)—or indeed been lost—from human history. For Foucault, however, what is 'prescribed as thought' in all three movements 'is something like the "Same" . . . modern thought makes it its task to return to man in his identity' (1973: 334).

According to Foucault, the epistemological impasse of the Classical Age is the inability to satisfactorily situate man as the point of the mediation of nature as God's book, and to account for the representations of the divine by the human. With the Modern Age, the problem has now become one of the status and reliability of man's account of himself and his relation to the world, and the grounds on which it rests. In short, what distinguishes the Classical from the Modern Age is the epistemological, social and political roles taken on by the human sciences and, more generally, human discourse. In *The Birth of the Clinic*, Foucault refers to the late eighteenth and nineteenth centuries as a 'chronological threshold' in which:

> illness, counter-nature, death . . . the whole underside of disease came to light . . . What was fundamentally invisible is suddenly offered to the brightness of the gaze . . . It is as if for the first time for thousands of years, doctors, free at last of theories and chimeras, agreed to approach the object of their experience with the purity of an unprejudiced gaze. But the analysis must be turned around: it is the forms of visibility that have changed; the new medical spirit . . . cannot be ascribed to an act of . . . epistemological purification; it is nothing more than a syntactical reorganization of disease in which the limits of the visible and the invisible follow a new pattern; the abyss beneath illness, which was the illness itself, has emerged into the light of language (1975: 195).

Foucault provides an account of the various ways in which the incipient field of modern medicine brought to light illness, disease, epidemics, contagions and ill-health, and dealt with them. This involved formulating new practices of spatialisation (of the wards of hospitals, but also of the body and, in a more abstract sense, of the space between diseases on a grid or classificatory system) and forms of visualisation (the precise and careful gaze, the microscopic observation, an objectivity and density of perception), as well as developing models and formulae for ordering, classifying, addressing and policing patients. The idea was to produce a system of identification, analysis, evaluation, treatment and control that made both medical practitioner and patient irrelevant—the medical gaze effectively abstracts the doctor, who in turn abstracts the patient. As Foucault writes, the newly emerging clinic constitutes both a 'carving up' of things and the principle of their verbalisation in a form which we have been accustomed to recognise as the language of a 'positive science' (1975: xviii).

In *The Politics of Truth* (2007b), Foucault takes up the question of how to make sense of these epistemic shifts in a concise and highly accessible way. A particular episteme can be viewed as a 'grid' that consists of a number of interwoven systems, forces, institutions and practices, and of their relationship to each other, to their history, and to the collective experiences of individuals and organisations at a particular time and place. Foucault suggests a multi-pronged analytical approach to the study of this grid—this moment in history, or event, situation or community in its many strands.

The first aspect is 'the cultural and social structuring of the experience' (2007b: 131): psychosis may, for instance, be classified as demonic possession, as criminality or simply as an illness—and it has been so classified, in various contexts. We might be dealing with the same disease and the same symptoms or manifestations, perhaps, but it would involve radically different ways of classifying and treating the sufferer, and of course the different ways in which the sufferer experiences his or her madness.

The second part of Foucault's approach to analysis is epistemological, which involves the problem of knowing 'what is the group of institutions and practices that must be historically analysed' (2007b: 131). With regard to madness, for instance, we could suggest that what needs to be analysed is the group of institutions—including universities, hospitals, professional associations, government health departments, police, families—with an interest in knowing about, controlling and treating the mentally ill. The practices would include pharmaceuticals, therapy of various sorts, policies and procedures, as well as ways of speaking about and otherwise representing both madness and sanity in private and public domains.

His third aspect constitutes an analysis of the history of that knowledge: What have we known about madness in the past? How has our knowledge changed? How have new forms of knowledge entered the discourse? As Foucault's work demonstrates, the history of madness is both long and complex, and some of that history has laid the foundations for current knowledge about mental health. The field of mental health is a productive site in which to explore how discourse can work, and how epistemes structure different truths about human experience. The act of naming a wide range of states of being as mad or mentally disordered, which is a feature of modern psychiatry—evidenced in the ever-expanding list of illnesses named in the *Diagnostic and Statistical Manual of Mental Disorders*, Volume IV (DSM-IV) which is used by psychiatrists worldwide—collapses under one name a group of radically different states (APA 2011). The contents page for the DSM-IV lists the following categories:

- Disorders Usually First Diagnosed in Infancy, Childhood, or Adolescence
- Delirium, Dementia, and Amnestic and Other Cognitive Disorders
- Mental Disorders Due to a General Medical Condition
- Substance-Related Disorders
- Schizophrenia and Other Psychotic Disorders
- Mood Disorders
- Anxiety Disorders
- Somatoform Disorders
- Factitious Disorders
- Dissociative Disorders
- Sexual and Gender Identity Disorders

- Eating Disorders
- Sleep Disorders
- Impulse-Control Disorders Not Elsewhere Classified
- Adjustment Disorders
- Personality Disorders
- Other Conditions That May Be a Focus of Clinical Attention.

Drop into any one of these headers, and the number of mental illnesses expands further: for 'Schizophrenic and Other Psychotic Disorders', for instance, the DSM offers sections on: Schizophrenia, Schizophrenia Subtypes, Paranoid Type, Disorganised Type, Catatonic Type, Undifferentiated Type, Residual Type, Schizophreniform Disorder, Schizoaffective Disorder, Delusional Disorder, Brief Psychotic Disorder, Shared Psychotic Disorder (Folie à Deux), Psychotic Disorder Due to a General Medical Condition, Substance-Induced Psychotic Disorder and Psychotic Disorder Not Otherwise Specified. Multiply this by the individual headers on the contents page, and it becomes clear that psychiatry has committed itself to a very fine-grained approach to very different conditions that have still been collapsed into one state of 'mental disorders'. Yet there is little evidence that many of these illnesses exist as such—at least as discrete conditions. The DSM-IV states that 'there is no assumption each category of mental disorder is a completely discrete entity with absolute boundaries'.

Foucault suggests that, 'In societies like ours the "political economy" of truth is characterised by five important traits.' Those traits are: scientific discourse; economic and political demands; its circulation through social institutions such as education or the media; its control by political and knowledge apparatuses; and what he identifies as 'a whole political debate and social confrontation' (1980: 31–2). It is not truth that is under consideration, but games of truth; and Foucault's concern is not with whether something is true or false, but first with why we are so concerned with truth, and then with how we deploy the concept of truth in order to play the game of power.

Criticism, he writes, should be 'a matter of flushing out that thought and trying to change it: to show that things are not as self-evident as one believed, to see that what is accepted as self-evident will no longer be accepted as such' (1988b: 154).

Discourse

The practices, systems, spatial arrangements and forms of address that characterise an epistemic shift are made possible by, and produced through, a particular discursive regime that not only brings into being and naturalises a different world and world-view, but also different forms of subjectivity, and ways of seeing and feeling. For Foucault, discourse is more than speaking or writing, more than:

> a mere intersection of things and words: an obscure web of things, and a manifest, visible, coloured chain of words; I would like to show that discourse is not a slender surface of content, or confrontation, between a reality and a language . . . the intrication of a lexicon and an experience; I would like to show with precise examples that in analysing discourses themselves, one sees the loosening of the embrace, apparently so tight, of words and things, and the emergence of a group of rules proper to discursive practice. These rules define not the dumb exist-ence of reality, nor the canonical use of a vocabulary, but the ordering of objects . . . Of course, discourses are composed of signs; but what they do is more than use these signs to des-ignate things. It is this more that renders them irreducible to the language . . . and to speech. It is this 'more' that we must reveal and describe (1972: 48–9).

Discourse does not refer merely to the content of communication, but the ways in which communication, information, ideas and other sequences of signs are exchanged and signified. As John Frow writes, discourses are 'performative structures that shape the world in the very process of putting it into speech' (2005: 18).

It is important to note that, for Foucault, discourse is not the same thing as ideology. The term 'ideology' is often used to explain how power works to naturalise itself, and is often associated with what Marxists term 'false consciousness'. The principle here is that ideology generates illusions and distortions that prevent people from realising the true state of things. Pierre Bourdieu explains the work of ideology by way of reference to what he calls doxa, a term that designates how discourses, ideas and values are combined to make power imbalances seem both natural and inevitable: 'By using doxa,' he writes, 'we accept many things without knowing them, and that is what is called ideology' (Bourdieu and Eagleton 1994: 268). Typically, ideology is associated first with a focused effort to posit one perspective as natural, true and beyond contention.

Although Foucault's conception of discourse has some parallels with ideology, it is not the same thing. Ideology often depends on an opposition between true and false, and Foucault considers it more productive to analyse why something comes to be produced as true or false. He writes that 'the problem is not changing people's consciousnesses—or what's in their heads—but the political, economic, institutional regime of the production of truth' (1980: 133).

With *The Birth of the Clinic* and *The Order of Things*, Foucault proposes that to deal with discourse 'in its irruption as an event . . . it must be treated in the play of its immediacy' (1998: 306). What this involves is a method of analysis that is altogether different from what he refers to as historical commentary. Whereas commentary 'questions discourse as to what it says and intended to say; it tries to uncover that deeper meaning of speech . . . nearer its essential truth' (1975: xvi), such a method 'rests on a psychological interpretation of language' (1975: xvii) that plays on, through each and every translation of the sign, waiting in constant deferral for 'the decision of the word' (1975: xvii). Foucault asks whether it is not possible:

> to make a structural analysis of discourses that would evade the fate of commentary by supposing no remainder, nothing in excess of what has been said, but only the fact of its historical appearance? The facts of discourse would then have to be treated not as autonomous nuclei of multiple significations, but as events and functional segments gradually coming together to form a system. The meaning of a statement would be defined not by the treasure of intentions that it might contain . . . but by the difference that articulates it upon other . . . possible statements, which are contemporary to it or to which it is opposed in the linear series of time. A systematic history of discourses would then become possible (1975: xvii).

The discursive analysis that Foucault performs in *The Birth of the Clinic* and *The Order of Things*, as well as the earlier *Madness and Civilization*, constitutes a kind of structuralism—or at least something as close to structuralism as Foucault was comfortable with. The idea is to avoid both psychologism ('This is what was meant') and the mechanistic dimension of linguistic analysis that, for Foucault, reduces discursive acts to the question 'According to what rules has this statement been constituted and . . . according to what rules could other similar statements be constructed?' (1998: 307). Instead, Foucault is interested in the discursive formation, understood as a set of shared imperatives, continuities, correspondences, rules and relations, that 'at a given moment . . . govern the appearance of statements' (1998: 309).

The statement is a difficult concept to pin down, since the examples provided by Foucault (maps, the configuration of the keys on a typewriter) imply rather than specify what it is and what it does. We can say that a statement constitutes one of the organising principles for activity, and helps establish the conditions of truth, within a cultural field. Foucault elaborates upon the concept of the statement at great length in *The Archaeology of Knowledge*, and it takes on a considerable methodological and theoretical function—basically, it is meant to explicate and demonstrate how and why, at a practical level, discourse performs its work across different cultural fields and times. Moreover, the statement is a point of intersection and translation: it is the place where different discourses (say, from and across a group of very different fields such as medicine, sociology, economics and sport) are integrated together and rendered continuous, both in a syntagmatic and paradigmatic sense. Foucault refers to:

> the case of Natural History in the Classical period: it does not use the same concepts as in the sixteenth century; certain of the older concepts (genus, species, signs) are used in different ways; new concepts (like that of the structure) appear; and others (like that of organism) are formed later. But what was altered in the seventeenth century, and was to govern the appearance and recurrence of concepts, for the whole of Natural History, was the general arrangement of the statements, their successive arrangement in particular wholes; it was the way in which one wrote down what one observed and, by means of a series of statements, recreated a perceptual process . . . it was the system of dependence between what one learnt, what one saw, what one deduced, what one accepted as probable, and what one postulated (1972: 57).

In the second chapter of *The Archaeology of Knowledge*, Foucault (1972) puts forward four hypotheses, cognate rather than mutually exclusive in kind, to account for the production of unities across and within the multiplicities of discourses, statements and objects. The first of these hypotheses involves the acceptance that objects (madness, delinquency, criminality) are necessarily dispersed across fields and time—in other words, we could refer, almost paradoxically, to a unity of discourses being constituted by and through a series of breaks, transformations and even disappearances of an object. Second, he proposes that statements might function as rules or precepts that give rise to and normalise practices, so in the medical field, the use of certain instruments, the weight given to statistics, and indeed the exclusion of certain forms of therapy or natural healing, are derived from an accepted truth about what, at different times and in different places, determines and defines 'good medical practice' or 'medicine'. Third, statements might be grouped temporally, in terms of their point of appearance (or disappearance) or longevity, so the emergence, in quick succession, of a number of statements-as-rules pertaining to grammar or hygiene would not necessarily signify coherence so much as a relation based on the contextual logic of that emergence. Fourth and finally, Foucault raises the possibility of a discursive unity predicated on a thematics—for instance, he asks whether a theme such as evolution could, from Buffon to Darwin, and despite its transformations, work to produce forms of knowledge. He settles, however, on the idea that evolution instead constitutes a departure point with regard to 'the different possibilities that it opens of reanimating already existing themes, of arousing opposed strategies, of . . . making it possible, within a particular set of concepts, to play different games' (1972: 36–7).

For Foucault, *The Archaeology of Knowledge* constitutes an attempt to test these hypotheses against the multiplicities of history, and to confirm or identify the rules of the discursive game—that is, the 'conditions of existence' (1972: 38) of, and the relations between, discursive formations, statements and practices. There are three important theoretical issues in this enterprise, however, with which Foucault's early work fails to deal. The first of these revolves around the question of how Foucault is able to abstract and distance himself from the objects he observes and analyses; and, by extension, with how archaeology is able to position itself as simultaneously inside and outside the wider play of discursive formations. To some extent, the problem is that Foucault's endeavours and methods in his archaeological texts tend to replicate epistemological problems that he ascribes to the human sciences in the Modern Age—that is, what are the grounds on which he authorises the methodologies he employs, and the knowledge he produces. Second, and by extension, Foucault's identification and analysis of the rules of discursive formations offer no convincing account of their relation to everyday practices—in other words, the ways in which discourse (and its statements, rules and points of distinction) produce and maintain a world-view and a set of practices. Third, while *The Archaeology of Knowledge* refers to the significance of strategic moves and possibilities as determinants or factors in the emergence and transformation of discursive formations, there is no account of how this can be articulated back to any kind of cause (where, why and how particular strategies get deployed, what legitimates them or accounts for their success or failure) or effect (how the agonistics of discursive formations manifest themselves within a particular institution, discipline or field). In order to address these issues, Foucault's work turns, via Nietzsche's notion of genealogy, to a consideration of the relation between power and knowledge, and the wider role of the human sciences in socio-cultural politics.

Genealogy

In an important essay titled 'Nietzsche, Genealogy, History', Foucault (1986b) provides an account of genealogy that indicates how it might function as an extension, and a means of overcoming the shortcomings, of archaeology. Like archaeology, genealogy works on and over 'the field of entangled and confused parchments, on documents that have been scratched over and recopied many times' (1986b: 130). However, instead of looking for and identifying epistemic continuities, rules and statements, or the sites and moments of rupture and discontinuity that presage new discursive formations and ways of seeing, genealogy is willing to accommodate and live with the truth of arbitrariness, gratuity, confusion, error and above all else the violence and the exercising of power that is history.

Genealogy attempts to provide an account and explanation of the processes whereby ideas are produced, activated and dispersed within and across cultures, and over wider historical periods. However, it also addresses the other two issues that we identified as problematical, or lacking a satisfactory explanation, within archaeology: the relation between a critical or historiographical practice and its contexts; and the manner in which beliefs, rules and dispositions are embodied and maintained at the level of the everyday. To take the second of these issues first, Foucault refers to the 'complex course of descent' (1986b: 146), whereby the values and dispositions of the past (a particular idea of truth, a belief system, even a scientific methodology) attach themselves:

> to the body. It inscribes itself in the nervous system . . . The body manifests the stigmata of past experience and also gives rise to desires, failings, and errors . . . The body is the inscribed surface of events . . . Genealogy, as an analysis of descent, is thus situated within the articulation of the body and history. Its task is to expose a body totally imprinted by history and the process of history's destruction of the body (1986b: 148).

The body is central to genealogy, because it is the site both to which power is directed, and where it manifests itself. So, to take examples more or less at random, one only has to observe how, both in fictional or media representations but also in everyday situations, bodies perform naturally and intuitively their gender category, their class position and their place within a cultural field (as familiar/stranger, important/insignificant, culturally literate/illiterate). In television and film representations of historical Britain, for instance, one is struck by the fact that, no matter how anachronistic or inaccurate the representation of a socio-cultural context (dress, forms of speech, beliefs and ideas) may be, the depiction of class-based bodily hexis is utterly convincing. This is probably because class politics constitutes one of the great continuities of British life and society; it is a form of discourse and world-view that wrote bodies and provided the legitimate bodily templates and precepts (how to move in specific spaces, how to hold and orient the body in relation to others) for hundreds of years. This is evident in the manner in which lower-class bodies enact their deferment or subordination to members of a higher class (servants with their masters, craftspeople with wealthy clients), but equally in the way in which, as Bourdieu has shown (1991), the upper class manifests its superiority in an ease of movement and a bodily manifestation of relaxation, disinterestedness and, by extension, control.

In terms of the third problem of archaeology—involving the relation between a critical practice and contexts—genealogy offers the concept (although it is probably more appropriate to describe it as a cross between a set of techniques and a form of address) of 'counter-memory'. Counter-memory requires that history 'turn against its own birth . . . to master history so as to turn it to genealogical uses' (1986b: 159–60), and it performs this operation in three main ways. The first is parody, or 'history in the form of a concerted carnival' (1986b: 161), and involves the taking of a comic scepticism to 'monumental history'. The second is the 'systematic dissociation of identity'; the task of genealogy is here to 'reveal the heterogeneous systems which . . . inhibit the formation of any form of identity' (1986b: 161–2). Third and finally, counter-memory opposes itself to what Foucault calls 'the will to knowledge' (1986b: 162): this constitutes a questioning of the hitherto largely taken-for-granted status of knowledge as value, and by extension a willingness to challenge the sacrifice and enslavement of subjects to that 'passion which . . . fears nothing but its own extinction' (1986b: 163). What this means for critical practice is that, in its own sacrifice of the will to knowledge, it simultaneously 'loses all sense of limitation and all claim to truth' (1986b: 164).

Conclusion

The various methodological moves made by Foucault may sometimes seem counter-intuitive and particularly estranging—after all,
what kind of history is possible if history itself is suspect? Or, again,
how can we be expected to analytically engage with and attempt to
understand the world when the categories that constitute the world
are taken from us? The sensibility, as well as the method, behind this
move is perhaps best encapsulated in Nietzsche's hypothetical story,
in the preface to *The Genealogy of Morals*, about the man who, while
absorbed in thinking about the world, is brought back to reality by
the ringing of noonday church bells; however, by the time he is aware
that the bells are ringing he has no idea how many times they have
rung, and consequently what time it is (1956: 149). What Nietzsche
implies here is that, by engaging with the world as if it were a categori-
cal abstraction, we are consigned to lose or mistake any knowledge
that is available to us regarding the world. Nietzsche writes of having
learned 'no longer to seek the origin of evil behind the world', and of
transforming the methodological questions regarding the knowledge
of these concepts to 'Under what conditions did man construct the
value judgements good and evil?' (1956: 151). Foucault's methodology
is strongly inflected by this kind of sensibility.

We will discuss the methodological implications of genealogy
and its relation to critique in more detail in a later chapter. In our
next three chapters, we will consider how, in texts such as *Discipline
and Punish*, the first volume of *The History of Sexuality* and *The Birth
of Biopolitics*, Foucault provides a genealogical account of the relation between the power–knowledge nexus and the emerging human
sciences; the development of the reason of state and disciplinary apparatuses and mechanisms of biopower; and the emergence of liberalism
and neo-liberalism.

2
~

Power and knowledge

Introduction

This chapter provides an account of Foucault's work on the relationship between power and knowledge, an issue that is fundamental
to his philosophical and historical project. We will consider certain
key principles that inform Foucault's understanding of power and its
connection with different forms of knowledge, most particularly the
human sciences. We will look at certain manifestations of power that
Foucault regards as being historically significant, including pastoral,
disciplinary and biopower. The chapter concludes with a discussion of
the limits of power, along with the role played by subjugated knowledge and counter-memory in facilitating the possibility of 'thinking
otherwise'.

The narrative of progress

We can begin to make sense of Foucault's understanding of the way in
which relations of power and forms of knowledge have shaped how we

live by comparing it with one authorised narrative that has circulated within the west since the Middle Ages. According to this narrative, the story of the west over the last five centuries has been one of gradual progress in respect of people's rights, knowledge, personal freedom and standards of living. Through great historical movements such as the Reformation and the Enlightenment, the west has emerged with a system of government in which the rights of sovereignty have spread to nation-states and to the people themselves. This freedom has been expressed politically through the emergence of liberal democracies; economically through free trade; legally through mechanisms such as the rule of law, individual property rights and freedom of expression; and finally, socially via civil society, the public sphere and the free press. This freedom has extended across the cultural domain and is manifested in the clothes we wear, the books we read and the openness of our thinking, as well as our enlightened attitude towards people of different sexual preferences, class and ethnic backgrounds, and religious beliefs.

This narrative has been contested in various ways. A perspective drawn from Marxism has been that the relative freedom and prosperity of one class (the property-owning bourgeoisie) has been at the expense of another class (the workers or proletariat). Feminists, supporters of ethnic minorities and gay rights activists likewise have argued that these sovereign rights and freedoms have historically been invested in white, heterosexual males at the expense of others. And so one way of making sense of the progressive movements that emerged in the 1960s and 1970s has been that they worked to extend rights and freedoms more generally, and that one measure of their success has been the election of the first African-American as President of the United States in 2008, something that would have been unthinkable 50 years earlier.

Our interest in this narrative is in terms of how it relates to Foucault's theorising of the power–knowledge nexus, and the social, cultural and political work that this relationship undertakes. We can situate Foucault's response to this narrative of western progress by drawing on two scenes described in *Psychiatric Power* (2006a), the volume based on his lectures at the Collège de France in 1973–74. The first, which Foucault describes as being one of the founding scenes of modern psychiatry, takes place in 1793 when the physician Phillippe Pinel encounters lunatics chained to the floor of a dungeon out of fear that they would give vent to their frenzy if released. Yet when Pinel releases the lunatics, rather than attacking him they respectfully and submissively express their gratitude at being freed and embark on a path of cure. We can see how this scene supposedly demonstrates how a modern and humane form of treatment can provide a pathway for the rehabilitation of the mentally ill, and their incorporation into civilised society.

The second example takes place five years earlier in 1788. When King George III of England falls into a mania, he is confined alone in a room covered with matting to prevent self-harm. Two of his former pages are charged with his care and watch over him calmly, but also show him that he is subordinate to them, and must be obedient and submissive. Thus, when the king attacks a visiting doctor and daubs him with filth and excrement, one of the pages enters the room, grasps George by the belt, throws him onto a pile of mattresses, strips and washes him and changes his clothes; then, after looking haughtily at him, leaves to take up his post. Such lessons were regarded as part of the king's cure.

Foucault uses this second scene in order to reconsider the humanistic values associated with Pinel's founding scene of psychiatry. He suggests that the scene involving King George shows how power is deployed through bodies and spaces: the confined room, the strength of the pages, their careful watching and intervention. It also shows how power is exercised through the submission and obedience of one who, because of his title, might in another context be thought to exercise royal power over all his subjects. At the same time, this scene demonstrates a humane form of treatment through its concern with minimising self-harm, as well as caring for and cleaning the patient. And, given that Pinel later uses a doctor's report of this scene to instruct others about effective methods of care of mental patients, it shows that power works through accumulating a body of knowledge that helps to organise and legitimise a set of practices.

Principles of power

From Foucault's description of the King George episode, we can identify four key principles that inform his understanding of power. First, it is not a possession, but rather a relation. Second, this relationship is not essentially repressive—on the contrary, it is largely productive in its effects. Third, it can only be made sense of through its connection to forms of knowledge and discursive practices. Fourth and finally, any relation of power can be resisted, if only because it necessarily constitutes and reproduces, in that relationship, oppositional categories, dispositions and forces. We will briefly explain each of these principles and then go on to relate them to other aspects of Foucault's study of power.

The idea that power is not a possession means it isn't an object that is either held by, or part of, somebody or something—the President of the United States, a ruling class or an ideological system. In the time of absolute monarchs, the king or queen was able to exercise power because it appeared to belong to them—they had received the gift of power from God. But in the Classical and Modern ages, power belongs to no one. In King George's case, any sense of his authority is removed, as he is made to acknowledge the submissiveness of his role. As Foucault comments in *Psychiatric Power*:

Power is never something that someone possesses, any more than it is something that emanates from someone. Power does not belong to someone or even to a group; there is only power because there is dispersion, relays, networks, reciprocal supports, differences of potential, discrepancies, etc. It is in this system of differences, which have to be analysed, that power can begin to function (2006a: 4).

For Foucault, power functions in terms of the relations between and trajectories across and involving people, institutions, bureaucracies and various cultural fields (such as the medical and psychiatric system, media and business) within the state. These different groups of forces constitute:

a system of relations that is established between heterogeneous elements in such a way as to realize a 'dominant strategic function': these elements could include institutions, architectural forms, regulatory decisions, laws, administrative measures, scientific statements, philosophical, moral and philanthropic propositions etc (McNay 1994: 29).

The second principle of power is that it is not essentially repressive. Foucault acknowledges that in certain cases (slave or feudal societies, despotic monarchies) power is exercised in an overtly repressive manner. However, the narrative of western progress suggests that these directly repressive conditions have been overcome through the development of liberal democratic institutions, and because of opportunities for education and individual empowerment. Foucault argues that power continues to operate within modern societies committed to principles of rights and freedom from oppression, but in a different manner; as such, his interest is not in whether power relations are repressive or progressive, but in showing how power relations can simultaneously be both coercive and productive. Power is productive in the sense that it shapes and moulds people, their dispositions and values, and their practices. There are inevitably constraints involved in the process of power-as-production: standard procedures to follow, limits regarding what is and is not acceptable, and rules and conventions for rewarding and punishing good and bad work. In the case of King George, a power intended to produce the king's cure involved limiting his movements and punishing indecent conduct. Foucault's interest, then, is in productive practices of power, and the constraints and effects they generate.

The place in Foucault's writing where he responds directly to this repressive hypothesis of power is the first volume of *The History of Sexuality* (1978). There he picks up on the notion that sexuality in Victorian times was largely repressed, and that it subsequently was liberated only through greater knowledge and understanding of, and openness about, sexuality. This knowledge and sensibility were supposedly derived from ground-breaking and influential work in fields such as psychoanalysis, psychiatry and psychology, along with the development of technologies in contraception that provided impetus for the so-called sexual revolution of the 1960s. Foucault doesn't accept this thesis: on the contrary, he finds a proliferation of discourses on sexuality in the nineteenth century that made psychoanalysis and figures like Freud possible, and that made sexuality subject to various relations of power, forms of knowledge and regimes of truth. The truth of the subject was posited as being tied up with, and explicable with regard to, their relation to and place within a regime of sexuality.

Foucault's objection to this repressive hypothesis helps explain his resolve in distinguishing his project from studies of power that focus on the role of legal jurisdiction. For Foucault, such studies of the law inevitably involve some considerations of prohibitions and limitations, such as the rights people apparently cede to become part of the social contract. This implies that the law, in its calculation of rights and prohibitions, is inevitably complicit at certain points with the power to repress. For the same reason, Foucault is also sceptical of moves to transpose such elements of the law to extra-legal sites such as psychoanalysis—for instance, in universalised concepts such as the law of the father and the Oedipus complex.

The third principle underlying Foucault's conception of power is that it can only be made sense of through its connection to forms of knowledge and discursive practices. As Foucault writes in *Discipline and Punish*:

> Power produces knowledge . . . power and knowledge directly imply one another . . . there is no power relation without the correlative constitution of a field of knowledge, nor any knowledge that does not presuppose and constitute at the same time power relations (1995: 27).

For Foucault, discourse acts as a point of articulation between power and knowledge; this is where they are joined together (1978: 100). In order to make children's masturbation an object of concern within sexual discourse, as occurred in the nineteenth century, for example, there was a coming together of a body of knowledge emerging from parents' close monitoring of their children's conduct within the bedroom, and the power relations (between parents and children) set in place by this monitoring. At the same time, parents entered into a power relationship with the supposedly expert knowledge of doctors and psychiatrists, who were vested with the authority to explain what these symptoms of 'sexual perversion' in children threatened (corruption, degeneracy), and authorised to prescribe how they were to be treated. In other words, by making children's masturbation a problem or an object of concern, it became part of a discourse, activated relations of power and helped to generate forms of knowledge.

The fourth principle in relation to power is that, for Foucault, resistance is integral to power relations. As Foucault writes, 'there are no relations of power without resistances; the latter are all the more real and effective because they are formed right at the point where relations of power are exercised' (1980: 142). We can point to two reasons why power produces resistance. First, Foucault emphasises how forms of knowledge, categories and discourses aren't natural—they are part of the 'effects of power'; and one of the reasons that people are able to resist the forces of power is precisely because discourses and practices of power have to claim universality, while inevitably revealing themselves as contingent. Without any final authority to make people believe (say, an acceptance that God has authorised certain discourses or categories), the operations of power will always fall short of the claims that underlie them. In other words, there is no basis for the 'willing suspension of disbelief' that sustains power. Claude Lefort (1986) explains this change as a move from discourse 'on the social' to discourse 'of the social'; in the first instance, a few privileged discourses speak from an authorised outside, while in the second instance a multitude of internal discourses compete with one another. Second, because power for Foucault is essentially productive rather than repressive, the technologies, institutions and discourses through which power circulates produce an almost infinite variety of categories and sub-categories of people and forms of behaviour, which compete with one another to regulate and control populations. However, the production of categories of the normal, healthy and good presume other, antithetical categories—the pervert, the deviant, the homosexual, the hysteric and the psychotic. That is to say, all practices of power produce their residue that resists being recuperated into their field of operations.

Methodology and relations of power

These underlying principles informing Foucault's conceptualisation of power are expressed through the methodologies he employs in studying practices of power relations. Throughout his work, Foucault studied power as it was manifested in a variety of social institutions and practices: the pastoral care and confessional of Christianity; disciplines associated with training and moulding people's bodies and habits of mind—a practice of power that emerged from the seventeenth century; psychiatry as it emerged as a field of knowledge and practice in the nineteenth century; so-called biopower or biopolitics, which dealt with the health and security of humans at the level of population; along with liberal and neo-liberal government, which focuses on how economic practices have shaped the ways in which people have conducted their lives from the eighteenth century through to the present day. What characterises Foucault's method in each of these cases is the identification of the different elements that constitute those apparatuses, discourses, knowledge and sites—such as the psychiatric clinic, the prison or the marketplace—through which power circulates. These elements make up the condition of possibility for the operation of that particular practice of power. As we saw with the case of King George, these elements can consist of physical bodies and materials, but they can also be a particular way of looking, or an architectural arrangement that affects the ways in which bodies are gazed upon and made subject to the surveillance of others.

Such relations of power are not set in stone. Power can flow very quickly from one point or area to another, depending on changing alliances and circumstances; power is mobile and contingent. We can make sense of this characteristic of power through reference to factories. One understanding deriving from Marxist thought has been that the factory managers possessed power over their workers and used it to exploit them for greater profits. That is to say, the owners of the means of production also owned the power through which that production was generated. For Foucault, factory production was the effect of a disciplinary power that both shaped the workers bodily and in terms of their conduct, carefully moulding them through training and surveillance, and distributing them in space and time to be effective producers. The point is that while factory managers might mobilise this disciplinary power to facilitate production, the power itself exists beyond their possession or control, since it could just as readily be mobilised within a state-owned company or workers' cooperative organisation in a socialist country, or conceivably be used to subject managers to similar disciplinary techniques. So, rather than capitalism creating disciplinary power as a mechanism to generate its mode of production, we can see that disciplinary techniques could be mobilised to empower the capitalist mode of production, just as they could to enable practices associated with very different ideologies, such as communism or fascism.

Power: archaeology and genealogy

Foucault developed this concern with particular practices of power through the research methods of archaeology and genealogy, which we discussed in Chapter 1. These methods were important in enabling Foucault to shift focus from the wider social epistemological shifts that he explored in *The Order of Things* to a consideration of embodied practices. For Foucault, power is always tied up with bodies—in particular, with the body as an inscribed surface of events on which the forces of history are written. Thus archaeology can be used to analyse discursive practices at a local level, such as a timetable outlining the prisoners' daily routine in a particular prison, while genealogy works through the relations of power generated from these localised discursive practices and regimes (2003b: 10–11).

From a methodological perspective, this approach explains why Foucault was interested in uncovering often marginal and overlooked documents from the historical record; these contained archaeological and genealogical traces upon which he built his method. In drawing on primary sources, Foucault attempts to make visible the grid of intelligibility through which power relations have been mobilised in sites such as psychiatric hospitals, prisons and other institutions. Just as a map uses a grid structure to make locations and references visible in geographical space, Foucault's work makes visible the elements and forces through which power operates in institutional space.

This helps to explain the number of optical terms associated with the production of knowledge. For example, an academic essay might begin with an abstract offering an overview of the topic, move onto a review of the relevant literature, and draw on pertinent surveys through which key insights might be generated. Now, it would be possible to think of these optical terms as visual metaphors that provide a concrete way of making sense of the abstract moves by which knowledge is assembled and communicated. Foucault's approach encourages us to understand these optical terms as material practices, which is consistent with his approach of comprehending language in terms of discursive practice. Knowledge and discourse are material practices, and as such are derived from and embedded in power relations. In *Psychiatric Power*, for example, Foucault discusses how Pinel's work with psychiatric patients in the late eighteenth and early nineteenth centuries contributed to the classification of mental disorders and, as we saw earlier, helped produce what was regarded as a more humane treatment of inmates. Pinel (2006a: 2) writes of the great importance of maintaining calm and order in a home for the insane, and of the physical and moral qualities that such supervision requires. For Foucault, such elements are fundamental to the constitution of objective medical knowledge, since the authority of the medical gaze is conditional on a disciplined order, and a regularised distribution of time, space, bodies, actions and discourses. The development of an objective form of knowledge is contingent on a set of physical practices that Foucault seeks to make visible.

By focusing more explicitly on the concept and operations of power, Foucault was able to extend his understanding of forms of knowledge conceptualised in terms of the episteme in *The Order of Things*, the archive in *The Archaeology of Knowledge*, and discursive frames in *Madness and Civilization* and *The Birth of the Clinic*. Indeed, his lecture series at the Collège de France, published as *Psychiatric Power* (1973–74) and *Abnormal* (1974–75) can be understood as a return to the territory covered in these earlier works in which relations of power are explicitly addressed in the context of the assemblage of forces constituting the psychiatric apparatus. Indeed, Foucault comments in *Psychiatric Power* (2006: 12–13) that while *Madness of Civilization* involved an analysis of representations in the way that these produced an image or perception of madness, in these lectures he sought to shift the focus from such mental processes to a consideration of the apparatuses of power through which madness became intelligible as a condition to be understood and treated. He also comments that while his earlier work tended to focus on violent deployments of power, he now wants to emphasise the productive effects of power.

Forms of power

Having outlined the principles informing Foucault's understanding of power and its link with knowledge, and looked at the methods he employed in these studies, we will now consider in more detail the forms of power–knowledge Foucault covered in his work. In his studies of power, Foucault plays both the long game and the wide game—that is, he explores power in its longitudinal and latitudinal dimensions. In the longitudinal dimension, he is attendant to particular manifestations of power throughout history, and as such is able to identify how such practices endure for long periods of time, and also how they are transformed and take on new dimensions. In the latitudinal dimension, he explores how power operates throughout all elements of social practice, from very private spaces such as family life or monitoring one's feelings and bodily forces, to very public spaces such as institutions such as the global commodity market. In terms of the scope of his conceptualisation of power, Foucault differs from both a Marxist approach, which conceives of power largely in terms of political economy and class relations, and a nominalism that focuses on power in terms of governments and political institutions.

One of the most enduring forms of power through western history, emerging in Judean practice and continuing throughout the Christian era, was what Foucault calls pastoral power. This is expressed in the image of the shepherd guiding a flock, thus making sure that the sheep do not stray, that they are kept safe from prey and that they are properly fed and cared for. Pastoral power was tailored for a social context in which people accepted the authority of figures in church and state as acting as benevolent guides for the journey through life and beyond. For Foucault, one of the most important features of any power relation is monitoring the presence of the other. For example, one of the aspects of pastoral power as it emerged in the Christian era involved the injunction to know yourself by monitoring the movement of your thoughts, such that they might reveal impure desires and show the presence of the devil within. This focus shows how Foucault's interest in language as a material practice can be distinguished from the semiotic concern with the relationship between a signifier and signified. Against this rather static conception of language, Foucault is interested in movements within it that open up the space of the other. So what is being actualised here, as Foucault expresses it, is:

> the opening up of a domain . . . which is that of thought, with its irregular and spontaneous flow, with its images, its memories, its perceptions, with the movements and impressions that are communicated from the body to the soul and the soul to the body (2003a: xxv).

While certain aspects of pastoral power are still discernible today, the decline in the authority of the Christian church, marked by the Reformation and the eighteenth-century Enlightenment, entailed transformations in power relations. For Foucault, this transformation is encapsulated in the genealogy of the modern soul. He famously declares in *Discipline and Punish* that 'The soul is effect and instrument of a political anatomy; the soul is the prison of the body' (1995: 30) and expounds:

This is the historical reality of this soul, which, unlike the soul represented by Christian theology, is not born in sin and subject to punishment, but is born out of methods of punishment, supervision and constraint. This real, non-corporal soul . . . is the element in which are articulated the effects of a certain type of power and the reference of a certain type of knowledge (1995: 29).

While, as Arnold Davidson acknowledges in his introduction to *Abnormal* (2003a: xix), Foucault's reference here is the Platonic tradition that conceives of the body as the prison of the soul, Foucault's reversal highlights how this modern notion of soul acts as a constraining mechanism in relation to our bodily forces, shaping their conduct according to certain norms and standardised procedures. This conception of the soul includes the notions of the ego, psyche, will, heart and inner core or truth—the notion of a fundamental essence that appears as if it is intrinsic to human identity. Foucault is concerned with showing how this soul, far from actually being a fundamental part of identity, is produced through practices of power and knowledge centred on the body, and is part of the wider processes of disciplinarity.

Games of truth

For Foucault, power and knowledge are connected with his interest in the games of truth—that is, the question of speaking the truth (about our subjectivity, for example, or about the market value of something) is always the product of discursive practices. This is consistent with Foucault's general concern with denaturalising those things that come to be taken for granted in human lives, while also explaining why he was keen to distinguish his studies from those that were conducted at the level of ideologies, which for him tended to stand in opposition to the truth. Foucault demonstrates how the perception that a position, value, idea or narrative is true is a means of facilitating and naturalising regimes of power. This is evident in the production of expert knowledge across different fields such as psychiatry and economics, which are called upon to categorise and evaluate practices (acts of madness, the behaviour of the private banking sector), and to recommend forms of intervention (drugs or commitment to an institution, public bailouts).

We can identify the connection between relations of power and games of truth in the following way. Apparatuses and relations of power combine to generate certain conditions and bring them within a field of visibility, such as the conditions we recognise as madness, sexuality, delinquency, or economic crisis or recession. These conditions are then made subject to regimes of truth, which enable questions about issues such as the criteria by which it is possible to define someone as being truly sexually deviant, the apparatuses—such as the confessional or the psychiatrist's couch—through which it is possible to reveal the truth of someone's innermost feelings and desires, and the mechanisms through which we can discover the true value of a commodity within the market.

In focusing on games of truth, Foucault is challenging the idea propounded by Kant that it is possible to occupy the position of a universal subject who can stand above the fray of shifting and conflicting power relations, and pronounce a final and absolutely true judgement about what is taking place. Rather than being accorded the position of disinterested observer or commentator, subjects are always caught up in our position in the game, with its challenges, adversaries and perspectives. Thus any truth or right asserted from within this position cannot help but be bound up with the condition of the game, with its asymmetrical relations, shifting balances and struggles for dominance. Indeed, and as we shall see in Chapter 4, the abstracted notion of the market has taken an increasingly important role within contemporary regimes of value.

The human sciences

Games of truth have become especially important in the context of forms of knowledge, producing man both as an object of knowledge and a knowing subject, and using the human sciences as a mechanism for this production. The human sciences can be understood as those disciplines of knowledge that have helped to articulate the connections between particular apparatuses and relations of power, games of truth and discursive practices. They have acted as privileged ways of knowing that could be drawn upon in order to study the human subject at various levels, from the microphysical in terms of analysing psychological drives and physical components to the level of biopower, where the human is considered as a species with particular social and biological characteristics that need to be taken into account in terms of providing effective services in areas such as public health. The status of these disciplines as sciences afforded them certain authorised claims to speak the truth, just as physical sciences were presumed to speak the truth about such phenomena as amino acids, atomic particles and the effect of gravity on planetary movements. As Foucault comments in *Psychiatric Power*, 'knowledge of the kind we call scientific basically presupposes that there is truth, in every place and all the time' (2006a: 235); he points out that statements of truth are contingent on 'the instruments required to discover it, the categories necessary to think it, and an adequate language for formulating it in proposition' (2006a: 236).

Foucault has particularly been interested in human sciences associated with labour, language and life, such as the disciplines of political economy, philology and biology. He argues that historical transformations in these fields of knowledge have played a constitutive role in the movement from the eighteenth century of making 'man', as a working, speaking and living being, a central focus of forms of knowledge. That is to say, far from simply taking the human as an object of knowledge for reasoned reflection, the human sciences are actively involved in constructing what we understand to be human, and in activating a series of procedures and apparatuses of power for treating that human subject.

Rather than acting as generalised theories in the manner that has characterised physical sciences, the human sciences have tended to be calculated more specifically to provide and support a rationalisation for the effective use of practices that have taken 'man' as a subject of interest. For example, one of the first great human sciences that emerged with the formation of the modern nation-state from the seventeenth century has been statistics—which literally means 'science of the state'. Statistics provided governments with precise knowledge of the state's resources in terms of elements such as population numbers, the extent of plagues and disease, and the amount of wealth and natural resources within a state's territory.

This statistical knowledge has continued to be a fundamental aspect of effective governance of nation-states throughout modern history. As such, these human sciences are not disinterested practices that aim to produce a general truth splendidly removed from the affairs of state; on the contrary, they are closely bound up with the operations and maintenance of political power.

At the same time, however, developments in the natural sciences provided insights that influenced practices of power in other parts of the social body. For example, the scientific interest in the role of a natural physical force such as gravity that emerged in the seventeenth century was carried over to a concern with calculating the forces at the disposal of the nation-state, such as human capital, wealth, territorial resources and so forth. This is an example of the human science of statistics emerging in response to concerns that physical science has helped activate. Similarly, in the nineteenth century, Darwin's theories of evolution helped activate an interest in and concern about racial characteristics and fears of degeneracy, which then influenced the development of the field of eugenics.

Dividing practice

Another and related way in which power knowledge operates is through what Foucault calls dividing practices. Since it is impossible to make sense of everything as a totality, power needs to develop categories in order to make meaningful distinctions between things. For example, the academic field categorises knowledge forms in terms of particular disciplines, so we have the humanities and the physical and social sciences, and particular subject areas such as literary studies, biology and psychology. Within these disciplines there tend to be taxonomies or systems of categorisation for distinguishing various elements—in the case of chemistry, for example, between different chemical elements. Perhaps the key dividing practice with which Foucault's work deals is between what is designated as normal or abnormal. Indeed, in a debate with American linguist and intellectual Noam Chomsky, Foucault suggests that the definition of exclusion of the insane constitutes a malady with which contemporary society is still most afflicted (Chomsky and Foucault 2006: 58).

Such dividing practices operate throughout various social institutions such as hospitals (which divide the healthy from the sick), psychiatric clinics (the sane from the mad), and prisons (the law-abiding from the criminal). Dividing practices work to qualify or disqualify people as fit and proper members of society. Subjects are continually evaluated in terms of the normality or otherwise of mental attributes, physical capacities, feelings and attitudes, and sexual preferences. Disciplinary institutions organise their practices through actively producing identities or subject roles—such as the delinquent—who serve as the threatening 'other' against which normality can be measured. But the institutions themselves engage in violent practices. It is notable, for instance, that the four disciplinary sites to which Foucault refers in *Discipline and Punish*—the prison, the school, the army barracks and the workshop—all display characteristics that are closer to the terrors of the old system of spectacular punishment and torture than the new regime of gentle punishment and discipline. The scandal of sodomy and beatings features in discussions of the prison; schools (particularly boarding schools) are understood in terms of the threat of beating, bullying and buggery; and the scandal of bastardisation informs studies of life in army barracks.

Psychiatric power

We can draw on Foucault's studies of psychiatric power to show how the knowledge–power nexus has worked to shape practices that have had far-reaching effects on contemporary western society. Foucault has considered psychiatric power in various texts and lecture series, including *Madness and Civilization*, *The Birth of the Clinic*, *Psychiatric Power* and *Abnormal*. It is a key concern in his work in the sense that it emphasises how the notions of reason, rationality and sanity that underlie the operation of a morally and psychologically healthy and civilised society cannot be considered without taking into account those practices that fall outside their domain of normality, and that have been accorded a range of names and shifts in meaning: madness, lunacy, deviance and abnormality. In particular, Foucault is interested in tracing the various transmutations in power that enabled psychiatry, from about the end of the nineteenth century, to assume such a central role in determining the mental health not just of individuals, but also of society. This became evident in areas such as eugenics and social Darwinism, which held that the health of the social body was at threat from certain degenerate attributes associated with particular races. At the same time, psychiatric power moved out of clinics and hospitals to become generalised throughout the whole social body, affecting practices in such diverse sites as school counselling, sports psychology and everyday popular discourse, where it has become commonplace to hear references to somebody showing schizophrenic tendencies or behaving in a paranoid manner.

This complex history of psychiatric power has various genealogies. One is linked to the aforementioned practice of pastoral power within the Christian church, which acted on the model of the good shepherd guiding his flock and directing their lives. Through an apparatus such as the confessional in Catholic churches, and in some non-conformist churches whereby a person is required to provide an ongoing autobiography, it became possible to monitor the subject's movements, thoughts and desires. Now this concern with surveillance in Christianity became transposed into a concern with movements of the body within nineteenth-century family life. Indeed, Foucault argues that the modern nuclear family structure emerged around this time at least in part due to a focus on the parental role in monitoring children's conduct, particularly in terms of the perverse threat of masturbation. This threat was understood, in psychiatric terms, not as a sin of the flesh but rather as a perversion of the body and a signifier of degeneracy that undermined the child's growth into a normal adult.

Another important element in this growth of psychiatric power was a focus, in the nineteenth century, on the instincts. We have seen with the case of King George III how the madman presents as a raving lunatic or monster, threatening both himself and others. Around this period of the late eighteenth century there was considerable concern with the figure of the human monster who engages in activities such as cannibalism, incest and bestiality. This concern was popularised in both Gothic horror writing, and in the reports of sensational crimes in newspapers. It was embodied in the monstrous writing of the Marquis de Sade, and helped create the conditions for the emergence of human sciences such as ethnology and anthropology, which studied monstrous practices such as cannibalism in so-called primitive societies.

However, while the figure of the human monster exhibited physical signs of madness, during this period there emerged cases of monstrous crimes in which the perpetrators could not account for their actions. In *Abnormal*, Foucault refers to the case of Henriette Cornier, a woman who brutally kills the daughter of a neighbour, and when asked 'why' responds: 'An idea' (2003a: 112). Such motiveless crimes were disturbing because the new regime of the treatment of criminals emerging in the nineteenth century stipulated that no offence had been committed if the perpetrator was in a state of dementia at the time of the act; part of what makes a crime rational and therefore punishable is the interest or motivation behind it.

In the absence of such motivation, psychiatry acts as a branch of public hygiene in codifying madness as both illness and dangerous, so while the mad might not be responsible for their crimes, they still could be removed from society. Such a role afforded the field of psychiatry powers formerly attached to legal apparatuses in terms of judging whether a subject was fit to remain at liberty, while simultaneously enabling it to function as a medical science responsible for public hygiene. Thus the status, legitimacy and authority of psychiatry were predicated on demonstrating that it could detect a danger within certain subjects that might be invisible to others, but that could be detected through its status as a branch of medical knowledge (2003a: 120). Psychiatry was able to fulfil this role by developing a discourse in relation to a new domain of elements that emerged within its field during the nineteenth century, concerned with instincts, impulses, drives, tendencies and inclinations.

This focus on instincts and their possible danger then enables the concern with child masturbation and the threat of degeneracy that emerged later in the nineteenth century. In this period, psychiatric power established itself as a human science and branch of medical knowledge, and took on a juridical role in making judgements about an individual's capacity to be at liberty. In considering the notion of instinct within psychiatric discourse, for instance, we can work through the conditions of possibility for the appearance, construction and regulated use of a concept within the discursive formation of psychiatry (2003a: 132), and show how the knowledge this generated allowed a particular practice of power to take on greater roles and responsibilities within the social field.

The limits of power

We close this chapter with a consideration of the various ways in which resistance to power manifests itself and generates effects. Basically, all the relations of power Foucault identifies in sites such as Christian pastorate, the disciplines, the clinic and so forth produce their own form of resistance. In relation to the pastoral, Foucault identifies various forms of counter-conduct—for example, practices of spiritualism and mysticism—which challenged the relationship between the pastor-shepherd and his flock. Within disciplinary institutions, practices of delinquency constituted a resistance to the normalising forces enacted therein.

This is because, as Foucault understands and explains it, 'Where there is power, there is resistance', which plays 'the role of adversary, target, support, or handle in power relations' (1978: 95). If we return to the relation Foucault posits between apparatuses and the relations of power, we can see that the flows and manifestations of power are always both disruptive and productive; they produce a series of transformations, realignments, movements and responses that are sometimes radical and dramatic (the French and Russian Revolutions being obvious examples), but generally they are, to use Bourdieu's expression, 'more or less invisible to the cultivated eye' (1990: 155). Power produces both the organisation and inscription of things, and the evaluative and narrational relation between things; and it seeks to naturalise and stabilise what it produces. Resistances, on the other hand, are:

> the odd term in relations of power; they are inscribed in the latter as an irreducible opposite. Hence they too are distributed in irregular fashion: the points, knots, or focuses of resistance are spread over time and space at varying densities, at times mobilizing groups or individuals in a definitive way, inflaming certain points of the body, certain moments in life, certain types

of behaviour . . . more often one is dealing with mobile and transitory points of resistance, producing cleavages in a society that shift about, fracturing unities and effecting regroupings, furrowing across individuals themselves, cutting them up and remolding them, marking off irreducible regions in them, in their bodies and minds. Just as the network of power relations ends by forming a dense web that passes through apparatuses and institutions, without being exactly localized in them, so too the swarm of points of resistance traverses social stratifications and individual unities (1987: 96).

Foucault is not suggesting that resistance to one model of power relations leads to another more progressive regime. Rather, each transformation in power relations constitutes a different combination of apparatuses and problematic forces, with different flows and intensities between them, and it is the task of the historian to make these relations visible and intelligible.

Local knowledge

For Foucault, just as relations of power necessarily involve resistance, so too can forms of knowledge. In *Society Must Be Defended*, he points to the possible insurrection of subjugated forms of knowledge—that is, to historical contents that have been buried or masked in functional coherences or formal systematisations. These subjugated forms of knowledge are regarded as non-conceptual ways of knowing that are naïve, inferior and insufficiently elaborated, and below the required level of erudition or scientificity (2003b: 6–7). Foucault writes that in France during the eighteenth century there emerged processes that allowed bigger, more general or more industrialised knowledge, or knowledge that circulated more easily, to annex, confiscate and take over smaller, more particular, local and artisanal knowledge (2003b: 179). Foucault sees this as a period in which forms of knowledge—rather like the bodies through which they were situated—were disciplined, and subject to selection, normalisation, hierarchalisation and centralisation (2003b: 181). For Foucault, the university played a central role in these processes—indeed, the university's primary function becomes one of selection, not so much of people but of knowledge (2003b: 183). The concept of the university as an agent of transformation, within this function, is based on an active and ongoing commitment to marginalising certain forms of knowledge in favour of others. In other words, the university works to transform and mould the learning of its students and academics by promoting dominant forms of knowledge.

One element of the resources for resisting such dominant forms of knowledge derives from the history of political struggles and their deployment of what Foucault calls counter-memories, to which we referred in Chapter 1. This element is evident in his discussion of political divisions in seventeenth-century England in *Society Must Be Defended*. Foucault comments that this division or binary schema was generated in order for disaffected groups to challenge the power of prevailing authorities. These disaffected groups allied themselves with a Saxon tradition that regarded itself as having been displaced by the Norman Conquest of 1066. In other words, the prevailing authorities were marked as being the heirs of the Normans, who through conquest had usurped the Saxon race of their rightful position. Foucault sees the discourse of race, through which this division between the Norman and Saxon legacies was articulated, as being historically significant:

> This was the first time that the binary schema that divided society into two was articulated with national phenomena such as language, country of origin, ancestral customs, the density of a common past, the existence of an archaic right, and the rediscovery of old laws. This was a binary schema that also made it possible to interpret a whole number of institutions, and their evolution over a long period of history (2003b: 110).

The point is that as the Normans established their rule in England, they occupied central positions of authority in the royal court and the emerging cities, while the Saxons were displaced into rural areas. So the political challenge of seventeenth-century England represented a move to locate and resuscitate localised, rural forms of knowledge, language, customs and beliefs in order to challenge a field of power located in centralised institutions. The legends of Robin Hood and Ivanhoe were stories that those who constituted their struggle in terms of being the heirs to the Saxon tradition employed as counter-narratives opposed to the authorised narratives of power.

Conclusion

This chapter has looked at how Foucault has theorised power, how the power–knowledge nexus has been considered in Foucault's work and how forms of knowledge have operated in various sites to shape identities and to produce particular notions of truth that facilitate the work of power. We considered Foucault's argument that the power–knowledge nexus had to be considered as a form of cultural politics; and more specifically that discourses of progress, learning, scholarship, research, enlightenment and humanity were contemporaneous with a regime of techniques and practices that moulded, disposed and regulated people's behaviour and thinking. Foucault explains this development in terms of the emergence, in the sixteenth century, of what he terms 'the reason of state', which he understands as a sensibility that sought to maximise the resources and power of the state, considered as an entity of and for itself. In our next chapter, we will provide an account of the theories, ideas and apparatuses associated with the reason of state, and the concomitant debates about issues of governance, which also emerged in the sixteenth and seventeenth centuries.

3
~

Governmentality

Introduction

In Chapter 2, we gave an account of the ways in which the power–knowledge nexus facilitated the development of categories, apparatuses and techniques that were used for the categorisation, surveillance and regulation of populations. In this chapter, we will look at both the discursive and historical contexts that provided the impetus for these developments (specifically, changes to theories and practices of what Foucault calls 'the art of government', and the rise of the reason of state), and the concomitant development of disciplinary practices and apparatuses associated with the exercising of biopower.

We will focus on Foucault's work on police, disciplinary and governmental power associated with the reason of state from the sixteenth century to the mid-eighteenth century. In doing so, we will particularly draw on three of Foucault's texts from the 1970s: *Discipline and Punish*, published in France in 1975, in which he traces the role of disciplinary power in the birth of the modern prison in late eighteenth and early nineteenth centuries; *Society Must Be Defended*, the lecture series Foucault presented to the Collège de France in 1975–76, in which he explores the interconnections between the force relations that constitute war and those that constitute politics, as they shaped practices of power and discourse within modern European nation-states; and *Security, Territory, Population*, the Collège de France lecture series of 1977–78, in which Foucault explores the role of these elements in influencing techniques of governmentality from the seventeenth century.

Sovereignty, subjects and the state

Questions regarding what constitutes proper governing or governance are inextricably linked to the notion of sovereignty: one influential narrative regarding the development of power relations within the state suggests that the powers vested in the sovereignty of the monarch gradually became transposed onto the territory over which he presided and, as a corollary, these powers were given over to the people who occupied this territory to constitute them as sovereign subjects. This idea of progressive sovereignty has informed a philosophical tradition that can be traced back to Kant in the eighteenth century. For Kant, a sovereign subject is somebody governed by their own internal reason and capacity to assume responsibility for their lives, in the same way that sovereign countries are governed by their own internal reason of state. According to this philosophy, for a society to function effectively, subjects undertake to cede some of their rights back to the state in a form of social contract that enables one's own sovereignty to be balanced against the interests of others.

Foucault asks us to abandon what he sees as this juridical model of sovereignty:

> That model in effect presupposes that the individual is a subject with natural rights or primitive powers; it sets itself the task of accounting for the ideal genesis of the State; and finally, it makes the law the basic manifestation of power (2003b: 264).

For Foucault, rather than asking ideal subjects what part of themselves or their powers they have surrendered in order to become such socially contracted subjects, we need to look at how relations of subjugation can manufacture subjects (2003b: 265). It is not that questions of sovereignty and values attached to it, such as the rights of man, have had no place in modern European history; on the contrary, these notions were appealed in various reform movements relating to state power, parliamentary practices and fields such as psychiatry and penal justice. However, Foucault shows how such discourses did not establish an absolute point of reference for judging questions about the legitimacy of power within a state, because they were challenged by other discourses with different perspectives on calculating the reason of state. Foucault's focus is not on questions of the 'rights of man' and social contract theory, but rather on the networks of policing and disciplinary powers that worked upon subjects' bodies. Taken together, these networks of discipline and policing constituted the governmental techniques that shaped the sovereign subjectivity of the modern European nation-state. Indeed, instead of starting with the presumed autonomy of the subject able to draw upon internal mechanisms such as reason and intelligence to govern one's life and give it meaning, Foucault focuses on the relative autonomy of power relations that work across different sites and in different historical conditions to produce particular forms of subjectivity. This understanding of the autonomy and therefore mobile mutability of power relations underlies Foucault's conception of governmentality as a way of acting upon the actions of others.

The art of governing

Foucault argues that while there were a number of traditions and technologies of personal management prior to the Reformation (for instance the ethico-economics of pleasure that characterised Classical

Greece, the self-testing or *askesis* of the Hellenistic and Roman periods, the pastoral care exercised by the Christian religious), the conditions in Europe during the fifteenth and sixteenth centuries produced an 'explosion' of discourses, ideas and discussions regarding what he calls the 'art of governance':

> There was an explosion in two ways: first, by displacement in relation to the religious centre, let's say if you will, secularisation, the expansion in civil society of this theme of the art of governing men and the method of doing it; and then, second, the proliferation of this art of governing into a variety of areas—how to govern children, how to govern the poor and beggars, how to govern a family, a house . . . cities, States and also how to govern one's own body and mind. How to govern was . . . a fundamental question which was answered by a multiplication of all the arts of governing—the art of pedagogy, the art of politics, the art of economics, if you will—and of all the institutions of government, in the wider sense the term government had at the time (2007b: 43–4).

Foucault writes that, at the end of the sixteenth century, the fundamental point at issue was 'What is the art of government?' (Foucault 2007a: 237). This question was tied to the political transition from a notion of sovereignty connected with and authorised by the church and God to an expectation that governing and government needed to be driven by human reason and rational decision-making. There were two main factors that, hand in hand, facilitated this transformation of the apparatuses and logics of the government of the state and its peoples. The first of these was the development of systematic forms of knowledge. To govern the state well (that is, productively) and to facilitate its development (in terms of territory, military strength, wealth, skills and communication systems), there was a need to know what constituted the state. By way of example, communication systems are crucial to government, military action and commerce, so it made sense to have inventories of and statistics about roads, canals, horses and mail depots. Along with those inventories, lists and maps, however, information was needed about what state of repair the roads were in, how reliable the barges were, how long it took for a rider or carriage to transport messages or goods, how goods and people moved through and between towns, and where populations lived.

All this required bodies of knowledge—for example, in the form of engineering, architecture, geography, town planning and metalwork. The same kind of logic applied to the most important resource—the state's population. Forms of knowledge—especially the newly developing human sciences—were put to work to 'act on the consciousness of people' so that 'their opinion is modified . . . and along with their opinion their way of doing things, their way of acting, their behavior as economic subjects and as political subjects' (Foucault 2007a: 275). Foucault argues that the modern subject emerges from a set of historical circumstances more or less contemporaneous with the development of these forms of knowledge and their application, through techniques and regimes of standardisation and quantification, to populations. Disciplinary techniques were developed for administering 'large populations of workers, city dwellers, students, prisoners, hospital patients, and other groups' in order to turn them into 'manageable subjects' (Crary 1998: 15).

Foucault devotes two of the Collège de France lectures (2007a, 2008) to a consideration of 'the art of governing'. In these texts, he does not deal with the practical, everyday procedures and practices of a governmental body or apparatus; rather, he is concerned with:

> the reasoned way of governing best . . . I have tried to grasp the level of reflection in the practice of government . . . In a sense, I wanted to study government's consciousness of itself . . . I would like to try . . . to grasp the ways in which this practice that consists in governing was conceptualized both within

and outside government . . . I would like to determine the way in which the practice of the domain of government, with its different objects, general rules, and overall objectives, was established so as to govern in the best possible way (2008: 2).

Foucault argues that from the sixteenth century on there is an increase in the institutionalising of different aspects of government—for example, whereas pastoral care (caring for the sick and the needy, looking after the morality of the people) was once the responsibility of the church, educators and physicians, gradually it came to be seen as something that should be taken care of by the government. There was also a change to the idea of what constituted government and governmental responsibility; what happened was the emergence of a rationality ('the reason of state') that concerned itself with the question of how power can be exercised most efficiently.

This change in thinking produced two distinctive types of knowledge: a diplomatic/military aspect that concerns itself with external political security; and 'policy', which is understood as a set of technologies and institutions responsible for internal security, stability and prosperity. To this pair Foucault adds a third, decisive element—economics. This combination of forces and technologies was, according to Foucault, extremely productive. If the state's population came to be understood, first and foremost, as a resource, then the proper role of the state was population management. This required the production of forms of knowledge that would allow the state to analyse that population scientifically, which was followed by the introduction of policies that regulated behaviour (for the good of the individual, which, at the same time meant for the good of the state): these both kept the population relatively healthy and productive and disposed them to incorporate and accept other forms of state intervention.

This new type of power associated with sustaining the reason of state and the security of the emerging nation-states of Europe is what Foucault understands as modern governmentality. He defines this as:

the ensemble formed by institutions, procedures, analyses and reflections, calculations and tactics that allow the exercise of this very specific, albeit very complex power that has the population as its target, the political economy as its major form of knowledge and apparatuses of security as its essential technical instrument (2007a: 108).

This form of governmentality has been significant historically in making this form of power pre-eminent over other types associated with sovereignty and disciplines, for example. It brought about a shift from the state of justice of the Middle Ages to the administrative state that emerged from the fifteenth century, and still is the model of government we find throughout western society today (2007a: 108). It involves a mutation and transformation in technologies of power from sovereignty and discipline to apparatuses of security associated with the reason of state. This transformation created the conditions of possibility for the emergence of fields of political science and political economy as integral elements of the rational calculations of liberal governmentality. And one effect of this transformation has been not so much to eliminate other technologies of power associated with sovereignty and discipline as to change their focus: to establish what institutional form and legal basis might be accorded questions of sovereignty within the modern state (2007a: 106), and what role disciplinary apparatuses might play in the service of this goal to manage population effectively and in depth, in all its fine points and details (2007a: 107).

Foucault's work on governmentality marks the ways in which power is diffused from a relatively closed space of disciplinary institutions like the prison and school to the more open space of general society. This diffusion of power is a significant factor in producing what Foucault's philosophical contemporary, Gilles Deleuze, calls 'control societies', which operate not by confining people, but through continuous control and instant communication (Foucault 1995: 174).

Such societies are characterised by 'electronic tagging' in penal practice, continuous assessment in the school system, open hospitals and teams providing home care, and continual training and continual monitoring in workplaces.

The reason of state

The reason of state became a particularly significant concern within modern Europe from the late sixteenth and seventeenth centuries. Indeed, the system of modern nation-states that we recognise as characteristic of the global community today emerged with the signing of the Peace Treaty of Westphalia in 1648, bringing the end to the Thirty Years' War, which had begun as a local German conflict and grown into a European war. At stake in the war was the Counter-Reformation movement, intended to reassert the power of the Catholic Church in the wake of the Protestant Reformation across Northern Europe during the sixteenth century. At the same time, the growth of certain states had led to imperial ambitions that were unleashed in the war.

The Treaty of Westphalia sought instead to place governing power under the control of sovereign states with clear geographical boundaries and governments that held the monopoly of force over their territory (Schirato and Webb 2003: 113). Thus there was recognition that the autonomy and sovereignty of states was distinct from the authority of an external imperial power like the Holy Roman Empire, and an attempt to contain the threat of territorial conflicts between states. While states might compete with one another through the accumulation of wealth associated with the principles of mercantilism, which focused on enrichment through limiting imports while encouraging exports, such competition ought not to result in territorial conflict. Competition was to be played out in terms of the ability of each state to maximise its resources via the reason of state.

For Foucault, a key element of the reason of state was its reflective practice: it was a term actively used by thinkers and writers during the sixteenth and seventeenth centuries in order to reflect on what might be the most effective way of governing a state and managing its resources and potential threats. Indeed, Foucault argues (2007a: 165) that the modern state was born when governmentality became a calculated and reflective practice, concerned with the ways in which people conducted themselves and one another. This reflective practice provided a discursive mechanism for activating relations of power directly tied to sustaining that state in terms of its reason for being. Although the kind of state that emerged in this period took on different forms, from the absolute monarchy of France to the emerging parliamentary democracy of England, this interest in articulating a rational basis for state power was a consistent theme throughout Europe.

Foucault considers the distinctive definitions of the reason of state being worked out by writers on politics in the sixteenth and seventeenth centuries. Giovanni Botero, an Italian priest and diplomat, defined the reason of state as, 'A perfect knowledge of the means through which states form, strengthen themselves, endure and grow' (2000: 314). His compatriot, Giovanni Antonio Palazzo, in *Discourse on Government and True Reason of State*, published in 1606, called it, 'A rule or art enabling us to discover how to establish peace in the republic' (2000: 314). Philipp Bogislaw von Chemnitz, a publicist and solider, in *De Ratione status*, published in 1647, identified it as, 'A certain political consideration required for all public matters, councils, and projects, whose only aim is the state's preservation, expansion and felicity; to which end, the easiest and promptest means are to be employed' (2000: 314).

Foucault takes from these texts what he considers to be the constituent elements of the reason of state. It is an art of governing so as to preserve peace within the state through the expansion of state powers. The focus on maintaining peace between states entailed the development of a diplomatic and military apparatus, while the emphasis on growing the state's power involved a mercantilist concern with maximising production of raw and processed materials, and thereby enriching the state's coffers with gold and silver. Such enrichment was understood as an index of the monarch's prestige and, as a corollary, the state's strength.

The reason of state as it emerged in this period sought to articulate a relationship between the sovereign and the people that was based on calculating the relative powers of each party. For example, Machiavelli's *The Prince* (1532) makes sense of the state on the basis of the power of the monarch: the role of the state is to protect the prince's interests. Foucault's focus, however, is on the literature that opposed Machiavelli in the sense of seeking to balance the prince's power with the concerns of the people. The reason of state marks not only a political transformation in the development of sovereign state, but also a transformation at the level of power relations in order to generate an effective mode of governmentality. Pastoral power was reactivated because of its focus on directing the lives and conduct of people, based on the notion of the shepherd directing his flock so that it was able to stay safe and not stray off course. The reason of state sought to generate power free of the Christian pastorate, but with a similar focus on guiding people through their lives and governing their conduct to maintain good order.

There are important elements of pastoral power that enabled it to play a constitutive role in the reason of state. While from the sixteenth century 'to govern' acquires a specifically political meaning, before then the concept of governing covered a wide semantic domain concerned with such things as movement in space, material subsistence, diet, the care and control of oneself and others, in terms of body, soul and conduct, and an ongoing exchange and intercourse between oneself and another (2007a: 122). Foucault refers to texts that make sense of government of different levels: governing oneself (which is tied up with morality), governing one's family (which is associated historically with questions of economy) and governing the state (which is associated with politics) (2007a: 93–4). Understood in this way, the concept of governing involves thinking through lines of descent between distinct levels of government (in what ways can governing the state act as a model for governing oneself and one's family?) as well as lines of ascent. This is evident in the way displacing a concern with economy from the family to the state makes possible the development of mechanisms of the modern political economy, while also establishing a condition in which the family constitutes a key site within this form of government. Pastoral power was integral to this practice of governing in the sense that the shepherd's power is essentially exercised over a multiplicity in movement, his flock (2007a: 125). At the same time, throughout Christianity the pastorate remained distinct from political power (2007a: 154). That meant it was distinguished from the negative connotations associated with the Holy Roman Empire and the Counter-Reformation, from which the modern reason of state was seeking to distinguish itself.

Policing

As pastoral power was reactivated in the emerging nation-states of sixteenth- and seventeenth-century Europe, it shifted from acting as support to Christian rule to becoming a set of relations aimed at the effective policing of society. Such reactivation was possible because the broad understanding of governing practised within the pastorate fitted in quite precisely with the range of activities covered by the domain of policing as it emerged in many European states in this period. This extension of police powers is indicated by the shift in definition of the term. In the fifteenth and sixteenth centuries, the term 'police' refers to a form of community or association governed by a public authority, as well as the set of actions that direct this community (2007a: 312–13). From the seventeenth century, however, it assumes a more mercantilist meaning connected with the set of means through which the state's forces can be increased while maintaining good public order. This understanding links to the idea that while nature can provide being, it is discipline and the arts that produce well-being, so the objective of policing extends over everything that provides for this well-being (2007a: 328). The sense of well-being as an extension beyond nature means that policing agents might be most effective within the artificial space of the city, and play a constitutive role in the construction of towns and cities; hence Paris became regarded as the first city in the world in the seventeenth century due to the perfection of its police (2007b: 336).

Foucault draws upon a number of texts from this period in outlining the range and role of police powers. One of the basic texts of the practice of police in France and Germany throughout the eighteenth century—Delamare's compendium—specifies thirteen domains with which police must be concerned: religion, morals, health and subsistence, public peace, the care of buildings, squares and highways, the sciences and the liberal arts, commerce, manufacture and the mechanical arts, servants and labourers, the theatre and games, and finally the care and discipline of the poor (2007a: 334). Delamare explains this intensity and extensiveness of focus thus: 'The police sees to everything pertaining to men's happiness' (2000: 320). In this sense, it is evident that policing was focused on effective governing of almost the entire range of activities through which people lived and interacted: being concerned with goodness, preservation, convenience and pleasures of life, as well as the coexistence and circulation of people and goods in relation to one another (2007a: 335). Policing in this sense assumes a role formerly occupied by the church in seeking to maintain a particular practice of modesty, charity, loyalty, industry and domestic order in the people, while also being interested in their economic activities and welfare—the number of people, their immediate necessities, the circulation of goods as the product of people's activity.

Policing looked back to pastoral power in terms of drawing on mechanisms that governed people's movement through life at a very intense level of control, thus extending the reason of state and governmental power into new domains. However, in focusing on people's well-being and happiness, it also anticipated subsequent developments in power relations associated with utilitarianism and liberalism. Foucault turns to a German text, Johann Heinrich Gottlob von Justi's *Elements of Police*, which highlights this paradox of police role: the police are what enables the state to increase its power and exert its strength to the full; on the other hand, the police have to keep the citizens happy in terms of survival, life and improved living (2000: 322). This points to two aims of, and tensions within, the modern art of government: reconciling the development of those elements constitutive of individuals' lives with the increasing strength of the state.

These two aims help to explain subsequent developments in power relations that emerged beyond the police state, and which involved, in certain institutions, an intensification and transposition of police powers into disciplinary procedures. However, in other sites there was a loosening of power relations that focused on providing space for the free circulation of goods and people characteristic of a liberal model of governmentality. In terms of the first of these developments, Foucault comments that the great proliferation of local and regional disciplines through workshops, schools and the army from the end of the sixteenth century to the eighteenth century should be seen against the background of a general disciplining and regulation of individuals and territory through policing practices (2007a: 340–1). This proliferation of disciplinary procedures made possible a historical development that Foucault explores in one of his key texts, *Discipline and Punish: The Birth of the Prison* (1995).

Prisons and discipline

Disciplinary power, along with its accompanying discourses and techniques, progressively colonised sites such as workshops, schools and army barracks along with the subject bodies that occupied them.

Basically, disciplinary power mobilises practices of subjugation and coercion that manufacture individual subjects through an anatomical politics, a microphysics of power. That is, an individual body is moulded through an intense regime of training and surveillance into a docile subject who is amenable to being manipulated into habits of industriousness that suit the economic and social interests of the nation-state. Foucault emphasises that this was not a unified, coherent project or deliberate policy; rather, it happened piecemeal, being evident early on in some areas and slower to emerge in others. For Foucault, the development of the prison system in the eighteenth and nineteenth centuries was a particularly rich site in which to see the emergence of disciplinary forces. The prison emerged as a central institution in society because it was a site in which the coercive force of disciplinary power could be used in a direct and overt way. As offenders against the values of society, prisoners could legitimately be regarded as subject bodies upon which the disciplinary forces of society could be imposed. So the supposed rehabilitation of prisoners involved them being coerced, monitored, trained, made to perform routine tasks in a repetitive manner, subject to various tests and psychological studies, and repeatedly questioned about their behaviours, attitudes and values.

This is where Foucault's project is distinguished from others that focus on juridical reform as the driver of historical change in modern European history. Foucault notes the discourse of reforming jurists, who saw in the prison opportunities for more humane treatment of prisoners than was evident in the old systems of torture and public execution. However, he shows how this program of reform effectively was undermined by the actual techniques of coercion and 'gentle punishment' that emerged in the prison, and took the body as a legitimate site to be manipulated and re-formed into a docile and compliant model of subjectivity.

A great deal of effort (discursive and otherwise) was expended on finding out how prisons could treat their inmates most effectively.

Plans were drawn up for regulating the space of prisoners, isolating them from one another in cells, or giving them different tasks dependent on such factors as their time of incarceration or severity of offence. A whole array of machinery was created to work through the prisoners' bodies. Prisoners had to operate treadmills, were drilled in labour gangs and on parade grounds, were subject to routine checks and physical examinations, and were required to perform menial tasks such as mopping floors.

The prison basically became a micro-society within the larger society. It had its own experts, hierarchies, ranks and networks, and its own codes of conduct, discursive practices, protocols and procedures. For instance, it had an internal legal system that could punish prisoners and add years to their sentence, or alternatively reward good behaviour with special favours and early parole. Prisoners themselves developed their own legal codes, so that people convicted of crimes considered particularly vile could be subjected to beatings from other prisoners.

The prison also created its own fields of knowledge (such as criminology and phrenology, which held that studies of skulls could reveal, among other things, whether a person was predestined towards criminal conduct), while at the same time providing a focus for emerging fields of knowledge such as psychology and sociology. Indeed, as a closed disciplinary institution and micro-society, the prison provided impetus for the growth of the human sciences throughout the nineteenth century, as well as for their challenge of the authority of juridical law and models of sovereignty. As Foucault comments in *Society Must Be Defended*:

> The discourse of disciplines is about a rule, not a juridical rule derived from sovereignty, but a discourse about . . . a norm. Disciplines will define not a code of law, but a code of normalization, and they will necessarily refer to a theoretical horizon that is not the edifice of law, but the field of the human sciences [with a jurisprudence of clinical knowledge] (2003b: 38).

As well as being a micro-society, the prison provided a model for the rest of society. In its dense web of disciplinary coercions, the prison developed and used procedures that, with modification, could be adopted in other fields. Foucault calls this trend of penal procedures moving into and colonising the wider society a 'carceral continuum' (1995: 297), and he mentions factories, schools and military barracks as being particularly influenced by the disciplinary techniques devised in the prison. But we could go further and note how these coercive forces occur, in various ways, throughout the social body: sports and family life, religion, and systems of transport and communication all discipline the people in these institutions, organising their behaviour and regulating the place of bodies by the way they structure time, space and relations.

Disciplinarity

In terms of this wider dispersal of disciplinary mechanisms throughout the social body, a key feature is discipline's concerns with producing docile, healthy bodies that can be utilised in work and regulated in terms of time and space. In an institution such as a school, for instance, a timetable regulates students' and teachers' work patterns by structuring their time so that they move from one set of skills to another throughout the day. We can see how space can be used to regulate people by thinking of the way a factory constructs different spaces— such as the different areas of an assembly line—in which people work, each person with their own tasks requiring particular skills and conferring a particular rank (floor manager, head machinist, boltcutter). The staff can, of course, move (or be moved) from one place to another on the assembly line, depending on the needs of the institution and the abilities of the people concerned, and with each move their position in the literal and metaphorical space of the institution changes. Thus disciplinary power accords a person a space within an institution and a rank within a system. Such ranking enables an institution to regulate both the movement of people throughout its space and the progress they can make from one task to another. In this way, discipline individualises bodies by providing them with a location that does not give them a fixed position, but distributes them and circulates them in a network of relations, and in terms of time and space.

The arbitrary character of the exercise of disciplinary power can be demonstrated by considering the forms of conduct it authorises in particular spaces. For example, one of the ways in which schools discipline students is by monitoring their form of dress. Thus it is considered not merely legitimate, but also necessary, for a teacher to make a class line up before being admitted to a classroom, and then walk down that line observing the students' bodies closely to check that uniforms are being worn 'correctly', shirts are tucked in, socks pulled up and so forth. But such behaviour in another social setting—say, making diners line up outside for inspection before being admitted to a restaurant, or treating guests in this way when they are invited to a dinner party at your house—would be considered an affront, and might lead to physical assault or allegations of sexual harassment. In other words, the exercise of power is arbitrary and contingent, and draws its authority and appropriateness from the situation or context is which it operates.

Foucault stresses that such discipline was not simply imposed from above. Rather, people submitted themselves to be able to operate effectively in the new social and economic conditions that were emerging in Europe during the eighteenth and nineteenth centuries. The new demands of factory production meant that people had to acquire the skills necessary to operate machinery, to manipulate implements and to endure the long days spent in gruelling conditions. A relevant comparison would be with an aspiring guitarist who is prepared to give up time willingly to long, arduous, often repetitive and physically demanding practice in order to master the discipline. Discipline worked through such a system of punishment and gratification. People could be punished, or they could punish themselves through a strict regime of exercise for various indiscretions (such as getting a chord wrong); at the same time, through disciplinary work it was possible to gain rewards and move up the scale—in this example, becoming recognised as a leading guitarist who could trade this ability for rewards in terms of both money and fame.

Normalisation

Another way in which penal disciplines have influenced the wider society has been via their focus on norms. In Chapter 2, we focused on the role of psychiatric power in producing the category of the abnormal, and this role extended to other disciplinary sites of confinement, such as the prison. Prisons set up ranges of procedures that establish what is considered normal, and evaluate the behaviours of prisoners in relation to this norm. In fact, people only become prisoners because they have been defined as having violated some social norms: as abnormal subjects, they can properly be made the subjects of a fully coercive system. Indeed, Foucault argues that, rather than really attempting to rehabilitate prisoners so that they might legitimately re-enter mainstream society, prisons are concerned with fixing prisoners in terms of their abnormal status. Certainly, penal procedures tend to confirm prisoners as having a criminal identity. They do this partly by defining criminals not only in terms of the crime they have committed, but also in relation to their life more generally. In other words, what is significant about a criminal is their biography, in terms of how that fashions a disposition towards crime, along with their authorship in respect of that crime. We can see this process at work particularly in the case of serial killers or people who have committed a major crime such as an assassination or celebrity slaying. There is considerable concern with what it is/was about a person—their background, experiences, family life and so on—that (pre) disposed 'the criminal' to commit such a crime.

Penal procedures also confirm criminal identity because prisons are in a sense like factories, producing a brand of personal identity that is different from the social norm—the identity of 'the delinquent' (1995: 251). Because most people don't want to become delinquents, they accept the normative values that are supposed to make them 'good' citizens. Delinquency also tends to support the social inequalities that characterise most western societies. That recidivist prisoners (occupational criminals or habitual reoffenders) tend to be from poorer economic backgrounds is, in a sense, typical of a social system in which the economically advantaged are seen as normal and good, while the economically disadvantaged can be regarded as being abnormal and bad. At the same time, in certain cases delinquency can be an appealing subject form in providing a model of rebellion and resistance to the dominant disciplinary order.

For Foucault, disciplinary power was a significant force in shaping the historical developments of modern western nation-states. As we noted at the beginning of the chapter, the progressive history of western civilisation tended to be understood in terms of the transition from the sovereignty of the monarch to sovereignty of the people. Against this progressive vision of history, Foucault highlights three interconnected transformations that disciplinary power helped to generate, which marked the genealogy of this sovereign subject: from a macrophysics of power to a microphysics; from a concern with spectacle to a focus on surveillance; and from an ascending individualism to a descending individualism.

From macrophysics to microphysics

The move away from a concern with the power of the monarch involves a displacement from a macrophysics that focuses on the absolute authority invested in the figure of the king, demonstrated in his wealth, grandeur and capacity to call upon the state's weapons of war and violence, to a microphysics that studies the way in which power circulates in a capillary fashion at its further extremities through the bodies of students at school, workers in factories and prisoners in penal institutions. *Discipline and Punish* shows how this shift occurred at the level of practice. There is a particularly horrific—and minutely detailed—description at the beginning of the book (1995: 3) of the torture and execution of Robert-François Damiens, an ex-soldier who attempted to assassinate King Louis XV. Damiens' body was slowly and deliberately torn to pieces in front of a large crowd. Today, this would be viewed as cruel and barbaric—as was the case with the penal reformers of the eighteenth century. But the punishment had its logic and rationale. Power belonged to the king, and when one of the king's subjects acted against him, the infamy of his crime had to be 'written', so to speak, on his body. Punishment, in this sense, was a way of signalling to, and performing, both the macrophysical nature of the power of the king and the consequences of opposing it.

By the nineteenth century, such spectacles of macrophysical power were considered both unacceptable and, importantly, inefficient as a means of punishment. They were replaced with an ostensibly 'reformed system', involving a microphysics of power that tried to measure exact but humane punishment for crimes, and rehabilitate criminals through ongoing training and surveillance. The point about such microphysics is that, because it occurred away from the traditional centres of power such as the king's court or seat of government, and because it involved quiet coercions written upon bodies and regularising habits rather than dramatic public events of the sorts associated with revolutionary political change, it tended to be overlooked. Hence Foucault's project of making such power relations visible and intelligible, of showing how the hidden power at work here was introduced in the name of the ideals of reform, but actually functioned to dominate and mould people in order to make them more serviceable for the state. What this involved was the ordering and arranging of every part of their prison life, so they became convinced that state power was everywhere and inescapable. Moreover, this sense of power insinuates itself as a disposition within the subject. In this way, they would become 'docile bodies'—not automatons as such, but subjects who were disposed to choose docility.

From spectacle to surveillance

What this shift in penal practice also involved was a displacement from spectacle to surveillance. The macrophysics of monarchical power involved the generation of spectacles—like the public execution of Damiens—that were intended to demonstrate to the people the overwhelming resources of force at the hands of the king and state that might crush any popular resistance. And the royal courts of European monarchies were places wherein ritualised displays of spectacle were an integral part of the power relations, such that courtiers and others competed for influence and engaged in various intrigues. Many of Shakespeare's plays, which themselves were written for the monarchs Queen Elizabeth and King James, sought to convey the spectacle of the royal court to playgoers at the theatre. Under the new penal regime, the focus moved from the spectacle of state and royal power to ongoing surveillance of the prisoner.

The most significant metaphor for explaining the relation between apparatuses and surveillance, Foucault contends, is the panopticon, which was designed by the English philosopher Jeremy Bentham in the late eighteenth century. Bentham's major project, associated with the philosophy of utilitarianism, was to calculate how the greatest happiness could be achieved for the greatest number of people and, given this, it is significant that he should have been interested in prisons. It tends to confirm Foucault's view that penal reform and prison development were central to nineteenth-century thought. Bentham's model of the panopticon was a tower placed in a central position within the prison. From this tower, the guards would be able to observe every cell and the prisoners inside it, but it was designed in such a way that the prisoners would never know whether they were being observed or not. The principle underlying the development of the panopticon was that prisoners would assume that they could be observed at any moment, and would adjust their behaviour accordingly. In fact, the panopticon idea was not implemented in many prisons, but Foucault sees its logic as an example of the disciplinary forces at work (1995: 203). In previous penal regimes, prisoners had been removed from sight either in dungeons or by transportation, but the panopticon worked on an entirely different principle—that the best way of managing prisoners was to make them the potential targets of the authority's gaze at every moment of the day. And this authoritative gaze didn't reside in a particular person; rather, it was recognised as part of the system, a disembodied way of looking that could operate as a general principle of surveillance throughout the social body. This logic of the gaze, like that of discipline, was not confined to the prison, but moved throughout the various institutional spaces in society.

From ascending to descending individualism

The surveillance generated through panoptic power marked a further shift, this time in the construction of subject identities from ascending to descending individualism. Feudal societies operated according to the principle of ascending individualism—that is, the more powerful people were, the more individuated they could be. Peasants tended to be grouped together as an undifferentiated mob while, at the highest point of the social ladder, grand displays of the monarch's power confirmed the authority and majesty of the person of the king or queen. In modern societies, which are regulated through the authority of the gaze and associated disciplinary apparatuses, subjects become more individuated the further down the scale they are (1995: 193). So the child is monitored through school examinations, employees through progress reports and the poor by way of numerous government surveys regarding their living conditions, moral habits and work history.

One effect of this descending individualism is that part of the pleasure of popular culture in contemporary western societies is associated with the desire to become part of an undifferentiated mass. There is pleasure in being part of a heaving mob on the dance floor or in the mosh pit at rock concerts, where bodies seem free of disciplinary coercions. This bodily excess recalls Foucault's point that one of the motivations for the abandoning of public executions in favour of a 'gentle' disciplinary power, with its accompanying mechanisms of descending individualism, was that the mob that gathered for the executions was an unruly—and therefore unpredictable—mass, which might just turn on the executioners.

Similarly, people who today are defined as part of a large group—'mass rallies' of demonstrators, 'hordes' of football supporters, or the seething 'mob' at rock concerts—are often depicted by authorities as being a problem. Surveillance cameras are often located at such sites in order to individualise these masses, to fix a name and identity to a person in a football crowd, for example. Indeed, such surveillance has become generalised throughout the space of modern cities. People in a city such as London can expect to have their image captured by closed circuit television (CCTV) multiple times as they go about their daily affairs.

Power, knowledge and associated forms of surveillance produce a complex play of visibility and invisibility. The principle of descending individualism indicates that people are made to appear as specific individuals, but the forms they take are dictated by the power–knowledge nexus. The ways in which people are made subject to various physical, academic and psychological examinations; the requirement that they carry identity papers; the fact that images of people's faces are a routine feature of these papers; the performance reviews that workers are constantly subjected to: all these are examples of the disciplinary power of the gaze.

Biopower, security and populations

In a sense, disciplinary power developed in response to the evacuation of sovereign power. That is to say, as the monarch's powers of macro-physics, spectacle and ascending individualism assumed less authority within the reason of state, disciplinary powers moved in from below, through an anatomical or body politics, to colonise those spaces now left vacant, deploying strategies of microphysics and surveillance in shaping individuated bodies within factories, schools, prisons and other institutions. However, such disciplinary power could not be totalising in the same way that sovereign power had attempted to exert authority over all of the state, since it tended to operate within enclosed institutional sites and was removed from other areas of social concern. Furthermore, we have seen through the execution of Damiens that an important aspect of monarchical power was that the king could decide whether a subject would live or die. Discipline responds by moulding subjectivities that can be judged to be normal or abnormal; however, that leaves the need for a type of power and governance that is concerned at administering and securing life at a wider social level, a dimension of the modern reason of state that treated people in relation to their collective identity as a population.

Thus Foucault complements and extends his studies of discipline with a discussion of techniques of what he calls biopower, which emerged from the late seventeenth and early eighteenth centuries, and focused on this issue of controlling life. Foucault defines biopower as a set of mechanisms through which the basic biological features of the human species became the object of a political strategy (2007a: 1). While monarchical power reserves for itself authority over who should live and who should die, biopower is concerned with ensuring how life might be preserved in the face of assorted risks and threats. The technologies of biopower sought to wrest control of those random events, such as epidemics or natural disasters, which can occur in a living mass of people constituted as a population, aiming to achieve an overall equilibrium within the social body that protects the security of the whole from internal dangers (2007a: 249).

The impetus for the development of technologies of biopower was in part provided by the great demographic changes associated with industrialisation and urbanisation, as evidenced in policies such as the enclosure of the commons that displaced rural peasants into cities. Furthermore, particular political and geographical factors played a part in the emergence of this more open and positive practice of governance. The intensive and extensive practices of power characteristic of the police state were more evident in countries such as France and Germany than they were in England, which had moved towards parliamentary democracy relatively early through the 'Glorious Revolution' of 1688. Similarly, as we saw above with the case of Paris being called the first city of the world, the direct forms of control characteristic of policing were largely a phenomenon of the city as it emerged in the seventeenth century, and could not operate as effectively in the open territory of the countryside. In the same way, the disciplinary forces derived from policing practices relied for their effect on being concentrated in sites of relative confinement such as prisons, schools and factories. In other words, the different political context provided by England, and the challenges of generating an effective model of governance removed from confined spaces of crowded cities and disciplinary sites, together provided the grounds for a different practice of power.

Changes in economic practice associated with the birth of the political economy constituted a significant element of this concern with security. The eighteenth-century French school of economists known as the physiocrats—so called because of their interest in linking economic practice to the physical forces that impacted upon agriculture and the productive cultivation of land—challenged the mercantilist emphasis on generating wealth through accumulation of gold and maintaining a positive balance of trade. While, for mercantilism, scarcity of a product such as grain represented a threat to the balance of trade because it required importing produce to compensate, for physiocrats such scarcity was a natural phenomenon that was productive to the extent that it helped activate an apparatus of security connected to market mechanisms that could take account of various factors such as climate, production, and the psychology of buyers and sellers, importers and exporters, thus developing ever-wider circuits of economic interest (2007a: 45). That is, by multiplying the factors that influence the production, distribution and consumption of a product such as grain, you broaden out the domains within which it generates effects. Thus, while discipline concentrates, focuses and encloses an artificially constructed space, apparatuses of security are expansive and concerned to 'let things happen' (2007a: 45) within a given territory. This move also means that the concept of economy becomes displaced from its traditional association with the family—relating to the father's management of the family's goods (2007a: 107)—to become concerned with the management of the population at large, in terms of their practices of production and consumption.

While mercantilism basically conceived of the people as a resource to be exploited in order to generate wealth, apparatuses of security concerned with managing population were interested in the people's natural productive capacities. That is, according to thinkers such as the physiocrats, the population was to be understood—like grain—as a natural phenomenon subject to fluctuations according to a variety of influences like climate, people's customs, material conditions, and religious and moral values. Understood in these terms, the population functions as a technical-political object of management and government (2007a: 70). It is at this point that we can begin to recognise the political economy in its modern form, constituting a new rationality in the art of government that aims to govern least but with most efficiency, based on an acknowledgement of the naturalness of the phenomena—human or otherwise—with which it is engaged. Bio-power, as a practice that sought to manage the human species in terms of its natural, biological characteristics, and which drew on the human sciences to do so, is a necessary corollary of this political economy.

It is in terms of the apparatuses of security associated with the political economy that Foucault understands the principle of freedom. For Foucault, freedom is not some philosophical concept or legal principle associated with the relative autonomy of individuals or the society of which they are a part; nor is it conceived in terms of liberty from some oppressive practice of power, or understood in terms of particular privileges attached to a person. Freedom has to do with the possibility of movement, change of place, and processes of circulation of both people and things (2007a: 48–9). Such freedom has to be produced continually as part of an ongoing concern with self-limitation, which is an element of the art of governing that Foucault associates with liberalism. And it was groups such as the physiocrats in France and utilitarians in England, seeking to critique governmental practice from within, rather than revolutionary movements that sought to overthrow the state, that helped bring about the shift that made liberal governmentality and the political economy possible.

Managing the population also entailed an interest in public opinion. The old public spectacles of torture and execution had intended, and often failed, to intimidate the people into quiescence: executions tended to be accompanied by aspects of the carnival, in which roles were inverted, authority mocked and criminals transformed into heroes (1995: 61). Apparatuses of security emerged in order to manage the threat of sedition, insurrection and uprisings. The revolution in France in 1789, as well as popular uprisings such as that in Tolpuddle in England in 1832, helped to make this concern part of the management of the population, in terms of another risk to be factored in. The dramatic technological and social changes associated with the Industrial Revolution generated conditions that sowed the seeds for possible unrest. Increasingly in the eighteenth and nineteenth centuries, due to the developments of media such as newspapers and magazines, an interest in public opinion became an important calculation in practising government. The concept of public opinion demonstrated that the people's support could not be taken for granted, or procured simply by displays of spectacular monarchical power; rather, they had to be catered for through the provision of services and support networks. The mass schooling movement in the nineteenth century was one such service. Public opinion functioned as another natural phenomenon within the population, which might be mobilised through various spaces such as street protests or newspapers, and which might be managed or manipulated for various purposes.

Thus an important element of biopower was the organisation of territory so as to create spaces for the flow of people, goods and services while also dealing with the threat of public uprising. Foucault provides an example from a seventeenth-century text by engineer Alexandre Le Maitre, who contends that a capital city of a state should be located centrally; be aesthetically pleasing such that it constitutes an ornament of that territory; must provide an example of good morals to others within the territory; and be the location of learned academies, since they must give birth to the sciences and truth that is to be disseminated to the rest of the country and, economically, act as point of attraction for products from other countries and, through trade, a distribution point for manufactured goods (2007a: 14). The redesign of Paris by Baron Haussmann in the second half of the nineteenth century, with its focus on wide boulevards instead of the maze of alleyways that had characterised the city since the Middle Ages, can be understood in terms of an attempt to both improve sanitation and ventilation and limit opportunities to construct barricades across streets, which had been a traditional tool in revolutionary uprisings. In this way, the Paris that had been regarded as the first city in the world in the seventeenth century, due to the perfection of its police agencies operating within confined spaces (2007a: 336), was transformed into an open, flowing territory that served the interests of biopower and liberal governmentality.

Such transformations were evident in the idea of the model or ideal town, which was not simply being dreamed of, but actively planned for and constructed, in the nineteenth century. While working-class estates within these model towns embodied disciplinary models that distributed bodies by localising families (one to a house) and individuals (one to a room), town life was also administered through regulatory mechanisms such as health-insurance systems, old-age pensions and public hygiene laws that applied to the concerns of the communities' population (2003b: 251). Foucault contends that sexuality became such a key concern in nineteenth-century governmentality because it exists at a point where the body (in terms of corporeal behaviour) and population (in terms of biological processes concerning the multiple unity of the population) happen to meet (2003b: 251–2). In particular, the notion of sexual perversion and degeneracy associated with the masturbating child, whose conduct it was feared would have corrupting effects on the health of subsequent generations, was a key element in linking disciplinary surveillance with the concerns of biopower (2003b: 252).

The escalation of governmental practices associated with biopower during the nineteenth century was a significant development of the reason of state in this period, playing a part in the colonisation of other territories as well as the political philosophy and policies of particular countries. Partly at stake here was the question of a state's legitimacy, which was an ongoing concern, given the declining authority of monarchical power and the growing significance of public opinion. On what basis can we say that power within the reason of state is being exercised legitimately? In certain cases, such legitimacy might derive from constitutional reform such as the 'Glorious Revolution' of 1688 that helped to introduce parliamentary democracy to England, and this principle was appealed to in subsequent movements for revolutionary political reform in France and America.

In *Society Must Be Defended*, Foucault focuses on another element that was deployed in this struggle for legitimacy—the concept of race. During the nineteenth century, concerns with history and race were taken up within the auspices of biopower, and became articulated with concerns about degeneracy. Through such articulation, Foucault contends, biopower inscribes racism in the mechanisms of the state (2003b: 254). This meant that state resources were deployed to counter the threats posed by other races within the state's territory—evident, for example, in discriminatory policies aimed at gypsies and other people without a fixed abode. It also meant that notions of race were applied to those groups considered abnormal, as in the concept of the 'biocriminal' (2003b: 258). Darwin's theories of evolution were exploited in the service of this racist dimension of biopower, which led to eugenics and ultimately to the state-sanctioned genocide of Nazism. It is in this sense that Foucault describes Nazi society as a generalised biopower (2003b: 260).

Geopolitics and colonialism

Foucault's work on the reason of state and the articulation between mechanisms of discipline and biopower has significant implications for understanding the relationship between different nation-states and areas of the globe as they have evolved throughout the modern age. Perhaps most significantly, geopolitical relations have been shaped by the long period of western colonisation of other parts of the earth. Edward Said notes (1978: 41) that direct European control over the earth's surface increased from 35 per cent in 1815 (the year marked by the Congress of Vienna which decided the shape of the world after the Napoleonic wars) to 85 per cent in 1914 (the year marked by the beginning of World War I).

This history of colonisation is significantly influenced by transformations within the reason of state with regard to European countries. We have seen how mercantilism involved a competition between states to maximise wealth as a mark of the sovereign's prestige. Since the Treaty of Westphalia limited the internal territory of European states, colonisation of overseas territory became a means of satisfying mercantilist ambitions. Thus many European countries were engaged in fierce competition to colonise foreign territories, and monopolistic state corporations—such as the East India Company in England's case—exploited the wealth of those colonies. However, the shift towards a liberal governmentality in the eighteenth century was based on the principle of mutual enrichment—the idea that, through trade, different nation-states could prosper alongside one another. An important element of such trade was access to a global market. Thus European nation-states might import raw materials such as cotton from their colonies, and in turn export manufactured goods such as clothes throughout the world.

When Foucault wrote about colonialism, he rarely did so directly—for example, there are no books of his on the implications of the French colonial occupation of Indo-China, the Pacific and Africa. Rather, he was interested in the way in which bodies were colonised by various forces, such as the disciplinary forces discussed above. Foucault was also interested in which discourses played a colonising role in ordering experience, making sense of these experiences and distributing people within these orders. Using the terms coined by Paul Virilio, we might say that Foucault was more concerned with endo-colonialism than with exo-colonialism (Virilio 1991): endo-colonialism refers to the ways an internal territory is colonised, while exo-colonialism refers to the means whereby other territories are colonised and brought within the control of an imperial power. These two processes meet in the age of western colonisation.

The endo-colonial forces helped produce a civil order and economic and administrative apparatuses recognisable as a nation-state. It is evident that the European nation-states of the nineteenth century, having colonised and disciplined their own people and territory, were equipped with the technologies, techniques and will to power to do the same with other peoples and territories, resulting in the great period of colonial expansion. At the same time, the task of pacifying, organising and regulating peoples and territories in the colonies provided colonial administrators and organisations with invaluable information and experience, which they 'put to work' back home in Europe. As Frantz Fanon (1963) points out, the apparatuses and methods associated with the 'treatment' of large groups of people (Jews, Slavs, homosexuals, leftists, gypsies) by the Nazis could be understood as colonialism being 'exported' back to Europe. Similarly, in *Society Must Be Defended* (2003b: 103), Foucault suggests that from the sixteenth century colonial practice exerted a 'boomerang effect' with regard to mechanisms of power in the west: while colonisation transported European models to other continents, a whole series of colonial models was brought back to the west, with the result being that the west could practise something resembling an internal colonialism on itself. This helped to generate the theme of a fear of racial degeneracy that enabled the mechanisms of biopower to exert such authority in the nineteenth century.

Civilisation and colonialism

The work of disciplinary and biopower that went on in producing a temperate social order in the eighteenth and nineteenth centuries can be related to the project of civilisation. The word 'civilisation' only began to enter into the language of Western European countries from the middle of the eighteenth century: it refers to the process through which a civil social order was being created in these societies. This civilising process was based on the development of various disciplinary institutions and modes of governmentality, associated with schools, workhouses, family life and so forth. It involved inquiries and surveys into the conditions and moral values of the people living in the emerging urban slums associated with industrialisation. For example, in England in the mid-nineteenth century, Henry Mayhew conducted surveys of the lives and moral conditions of people in the slum areas. Mayhew became a reporter of the underworld, able to distinguish various groups of criminals by the different terms by which they were identified.

This civilising project (or civilising mission, as it became known) had an important effect in shaping colonial practice in the rest of the world. On the one hand, it provided a moral justification for European colonisation. If the colonising countries could perceive themselves as more civilised than the people in the countries they colonised, then rather than colonisation being seen as a naked act of aggression, it could seem morally justified, even righteous—what Rudyard Kipling called 'the white man's burden' (1929). The overtly racialised discourse helped to implant the treatment of race as an instrument of govern-mentality articulated within a civilising mission. This enabled the mechanisms of biopower to extend their reach within the social body of the home country, as well as that of the colonised territories. Thus the theme of degeneracy could be projected directly onto the people from colonised territories as a means of keeping them subjugated so that their perceived threat of contamination of dominant races could be contained.

Said has applied Foucault's ideas to colonial practice in his book *Orientalism* (1978). He discusses how colonial practice was based on a construction of Oriental peoples as being less civilised than people in the west, and therefore needing to be colonised and governed by others. This discursive construction showed itself in official governmental texts, as well as in popular culture texts such as the novels and poems of Rud-yard Kipling. Drawing from Said's work, we can see how Orientalist discourses established a set of binary opposites, with the west as civi-lised, active, progressive, enlightened, the subject of knowledge, and individuals; and the Orient as barbarous, passive, backward, the object of knowledge, and characterised by tribal or mass identity.

We have seen how Foucault coined the term 'carceral continuum' to describe this process by which the carceral or punitive techniques of the prison gradually gained circulation throughout society as a whole (1995: 297). It is worth pointing out that this principle of car-ceral continuum not only circulated within the home country, but also became an important principle of the colonisation of other places in the eighteenth and nineteenth centuries. Indeed, the prison itself was one of the most important institutions involved in colonial practice. Certain Western European countries regarded the colonies as places to which prisoners might be moved, believing that by removing them from the home country, their corrupting influence would also be removed. One of the motivations for the American War of Independence in 1776 was settlers' dissatisfaction that British convicts were being sent to the American colonies. Having lost the War of Independence, Britain sought somewhere else to export her convicts, and thus ease the burden on her overcrowded prisons. The Australian colonies were settled by Britain from 1788 as territories to house convicts. Similarly, the French used islands in the Pacific such as New Caledonia as dumping grounds for their convicts. In this way, the carceral continuum progressed from the home country to its colonial possessions.

Thus the effects of colonialism on European states were several and far reaching. Colonialism helped implant a focus on race within historical-political discourses that related to the legitimacy of state. It contributed to a concern with the threat of degeneracy through which racist practices became inscribed within mechanisms of the state, both at home and in the colonies, by which people of other races or perceived to be a risk to the health of the dominant race might be expelled, excluded or, as with Nazism, subjected to genocide.

At the same time, colonialism also played a part in the governmentality of the European countries through its contribution to sustaining a global market, and helping to secure the interests of the political economy. Colonialism enabled European countries to mutually enrich themselves through access to the world market that it helped to constitute. Such practice also involved the progressive extension of the market into various forms of governmentality, a development that will be the focus of detailed discussion, exemplification and analysis in our next chapter.

Conclusion

This chapter has explored the elements of and transformations within different relations of power and forms of knowledge as they shaped nation-states during their emergence in Europe from the sixteenth to the eighteenth centuries. Foucault's work has contributed to making sense of the reasons, logics and rationales through which the forces of these states were developed, moulded and put to use. It is evident that this was not simply the product of ideological systems, but rather were material practices that involved disciplining bodies, securing populations, shaping families and developing particular forms of freedom and interests associated with the political economy. The development of this political economy from the eighteenth century through to today, in terms of the practices of government associated first with liberalism and later with neo-liberalism, is the focus of our next chapter.

4
~

Liberalism and neo-liberalism

Introduction

In Chapter 3, we provided an account of Foucault's work on governmentality, the development of the rationales and practices of the reason of state, and the rise of disciplinary mechanisms and apparatuses associated with the exercising of biopower. We also suggested that the logics and imperatives of the reason of state were forced to coexist with, and were gradually inflected by, politics and discourses of liberalism.

The development of this latter relationship has intensified over the past two centuries, and the logics, imperatives and practices underpinning the discipline-based reason of state have undergone something of a change, and perhaps have even been transformed, as a consequence. In *The Birth of Biopolitics* (2008), Foucault provides a detailed historical account and analysis—a genealogy—of the relation between government and the reason of state on the one hand, and the ideology or sensibility of liberalism (and later neo-liberalism) on the other. He traces a set of discursive and ideological developments that are of considerable importance with regard to the development of what we might call the postmodern episteme; for that reason alone, that lecture series-as-book could be considered one of the more significant works in Foucault's oeuvre. In this chapter, we will give an account of the main points and arguments made in *The Birth of Biopolitics*, and show how the developments outlined there presage and make explicable the capitalist- and market-dominated contemporary world.

Liberalism

Foucault opens the first lecture of *The Birth of Biopolitics* with a quote from 'the English Statesman Walpole, who with reference to his way of governing', was supposed to have summarised it as 'Let sleeping dogs lie' (2008: 1). These lectures are concerned with the contexts and factors that inflect the art of governing, and Walpole's 'Let sleeping dogs lie' story refers to the idea that good government is about never doing anything to rouse or antagonise the people. By way of effecting a narrative connection, Foucault quotes another story and comment that encapsulate the attitude of the commercial or capitalist class to government intervention in the economic sphere: 'Recalling what the merchant Le Gendre said to Colbert—when Colbert asked him: "What can I do for you?" Le Gendre replied: "What can you do for us? Leave us alone"' (2008: 20). This story introduces 'the principle of the self-limitation of governmental reason which all governments must follow and respect . . . this is broadly what is called "liberalism"' (2008: 20). Foucault argues that liberalism is not something that is contrary to or disassociated from the reason of state, but rather 'its point of inflection in the curve of its development' (2008: 28). So the various issues and topics that we associate with the reason of state, including the development of biopolitics, can only be fully considered:

> when we understand what is at stake in this regime of liberal-
> ism opposed to . . . or rather, fundamentally modifying [the

reason of state] . . . only when we know what this governmental regime called liberalism was, will we be able to grasp what biopolitics is (2008: 22).

Foucault argues that the reason of state was disposed to an accommodation with liberalism because of specific historical contexts and developments in Europe. He suggests that in the Middle Ages the discursive motivation for government in Europe was spiritual: the sovereign was charged, above all else, with ensuring that 'subjects gain their salvation: in the next world' (2008: 4). In the Middle Ages, each sovereign was linked and in a sense subordinate to the Holy Roman Empire (and its emperor), which was authorised by and represented God. With the reason of state, this other-worldly dimension becomes more peripheral: from this point on, 'The state exists only for itself and in relation to itself, whatever obedience it may owe to other systems like nature or god' (2008: 5).

After the Middle Ages, the reason of state takes itself as its main object, and consequently everything within the state (the population, material resources, culture) is to be understood and managed in terms of a utilitarian economics. This gives rise to two sets of institutions: for internal purposes, these correspond to the apparatuses and mechanisms of policing, discipline and surveillance; for external purposes, there is the army and the diplomatic corps. Foucault argues that from the seventeenth century, or at least from the period of the Treaty of Westphalia, the external ambitions of the state are subject to limitation; however, the consequence of this is that the object of what Foucault refers to as the 'police state' is 'almost unlimited' (2008: 7). The state, at least in theory, cannot extend itself (and increase its territories, resources and power) by military means, so the competition between states is to be carried out in terms of the 'economic' management, development and exploitation of the state's internal resources (predominantly its population). The mercantilism of the seventeenth century, for instance, is not to be understood solely as an economic doctrine:

It is a particular organization of the production and commercial circuits according to the principle that: first, the state must enrich itself through monetary accumulation; second, it must strengthen itself by increasing population; and third, it must exist and maintain itself in a state of permanent competition with foreign powers (2008: 5).

If the reason of state was already disposed towards a certain kind of economic rationale, then we can see why liberalism's championing of the market was not necessarily antithetical to the interests and imperatives of the reason of state. Foucault makes the point that another potential bridge between the reason of state and liberalism was to be found in the role the law and judicial institutions took on in the sixteenth and seventeenth centuries. In England, for instance, the opponents of Charles Stuart, and later various groups of religious dissenters, used 'juridical reflection, legal rules, and legal authority' (2008: 9) against the excesses of the reason of state; in such cases (and in France, where this line is taken by Protestants and other politically disadvantaged groups), the principle of the limitation of the reason of state 'is found in juridical reason' (2008: 9). Foucault characterises and contextualises this inflection of and challenge to the reason of state by liberalism as the development of:

> a new art of government that began to be formulated, reflected upon, and outlined around the middle of the eighteenth century . . . an essential characteristic of this new art of government is the organization of numerous and complex internal mechanisms whose function . . . is not so much to ensure the growth of the state's forces, wealth, and strength, to insure its unlimited growth, as to limit the exercise of government power internally. This art of government is certainly new . . . But only up to a point . . . this new art of government . . . should be seen as a sort of intensification or internal refinement of

raison d'Etat; it is a principle for maintaining it, developing it more fully, and perfecting it (2008: 27–8).

Liberalism and the market

What liberalism brings to the reason of state, above all else, is an ideological commitment to and emphasis upon 'the frugality of government' and a 'particular regime of truth that finds its theoretical formulation and expression in political economy' (2008: 29). Foucault argues that this regime of truth is predicated upon, and finds its authority in, the mechanisms, tendencies and rhythms of the market. He suggests, in fact, that from the Middle Ages on the market operates as 'a site of justice' (2008: 30). He cites four main reasons why it acquires this status. First, the market is subject to continuous and explicit regulation that is enforceable and enforced—that is to say, every market is characterised by a set of procedures and rules (as to what can be bought and sold, the costs and taxes to be met, the obligations on buyer and seller) that delimit and define (and guarantee) its operations and practices. Second, the market can be thought of as a site of justice because, theoretically at least, the sale price is a just price in the sense that it bears some relation to the work performed (the manufacture and/or transportation of goods, say). Third, the market ensures that everyone can afford something: the mere fact that the market is a distributive space means that it attracts a bulk of goods and services, which ensures (again theoretically) that even the poorest will be able to meet some of their most basic needs. Finally, and as a consequence of the preceding three reasons, the market works to protect both buyers and sellers against theft and fraud (if goods are of poor quality, they can be returned or will not cost much; a seller cannot be cheated of a just price by factors outside the market, such as physical force or political influence). Foucault writes that, in the west from the Middle Ages up until the eighteenth century, the market functioned as 'a site of jurisdiction' (2008: 31).

He suggests, however, that in the eighteenth century a significant change occurs with regard to the status of the market: it now becomes a site, not of jurisdiction but of truth. He explains this development in terms of two closely related rationales, both of which derive their weight from the positing of a correspondence not with human law, but between the market and nature, or 'natural law'. First, the market is seen as spontaneously facilitating the appearance and operation of a set of mechanisms that intercedes and provides an articulation between nature and the human; consequently, any attempt to modify or intervene in market mechanisms can only work to corrupt or impair them. Second, it is presumed that when these mechanisms are allowed to function, they will produce a 'true relation' between goods (and the work that produces them) and demand (and, by extension, price). This logic could be articulated as follows:

> When you allow the market to function by itself according to its nature, according to the natural truth . . . it permits the formation of a certain price which will be called, metaphorically, the true price, and which will still sometimes be called the just price, but which no longer has any connotation of justice. It is a certain price that fluctuates around the value of the product (2008: 31).

This move from a regime of jurisdiction to one of political economy is particularly important with regard to the development of the reason of state, for liberalism can now claim the market as the source of truth—and not simply human truth, but something much more profound and beyond challenge or argumentation. As a manifestation of natural laws, the market can be held up as that truth against which all government policies, interventions and practices can be measured. The market now 'determines that good government is no longer simply

government that functions according to justice . . . to be good government, government has to function according to truth' (2008: 32). The
advent of this 'veridictional market', and the consequent 'innumerable
intersections between jurisdiction and veridiction', constitute for Foucault 'a fundamental phenomenon in the history of the modern west'
(2008: 34).

The market and the law

The question of the intersection between the truth of the market
and the issue of law is central to the work of economic, legal and
social theorists of the eighteenth century; however, generally within
the terms of a specific (and liberal) inflection, the question is not so
much about how the truth of the market can be reconciled with the
imperatives of justice, but rather the ways in which public law can
be utilised so as to limit the intervention and interference of government in the market. This is what Foucault refers to as a 'shift in the
centre of gravity of public law' (2008: 39). Whereas the function of
the law previously had to do with the relation between the sovereign
and the issue of legitimacy (the basis of sovereignty and the responsibilities of the sovereign with regard to the people), in the eighteenth
century law functioned predominantly to set limits on the ability of
government to exercise power with regard to its citizens. This was not
directed against the reason of state *per se*, so much as against those
means that would constitute misguided and uneconomic attempts to
meet its imperatives.

How was this imbrication of the market and the law to be effected?
Foucault suggests that, at the end of the eighteenth and the beginning
of the nineteenth centuries, there were two main ways of resolving the
issue, one corresponding to the situation as it developed in France, the
other to that in England. The first, the 'juridico-deductive approach'
(2008: 39), which Foucault associates with Rousseau, starts from the

idea that there are basic universal (that is, male) rights, and that any attempt to impinge upon or revoke these rights by the sovereign is unlawful without the assent or permission of the people. As Foucault points out, this 'revolutionary approach' in a sense simply retraces the attempts of seventeenth-century groups to use the law as a means of limiting the reason of state.

The second approach, which he characterises as 'empirical and utilitarian' (2008: 43), starts from the notion that government—or at least good government—is defined by a set of internal limits that effectively are utilitarian in nature. In other words, if a government is to function in a competent, effective, useful and economical manner, and if it is truly to adhere to the dictates and imperatives of the reason of state, then there are areas that it should avoid, limits it should place on itself, and means that it should not employ.

How do these two approaches translate into legal practice? Foucault suggests that in the revolutionary approach the law manifests itself as the will of the people, and it specifies what the people have ceded, and what they retain by way of right. With the utilitarian approach, the law is a transaction that both binds and separates government and the governed; it protects the independence of the governed from the (misguided) interventions of power. The difference between these two approaches, as Foucault conceives it, is between the law considered as a mechanism for the enshrining and maintenance of human rights on the one hand, and viewed as a means of ensuring the independence of populations on the other. As he writes:

With regard to the problem of what we currently call human rights, we would only need look at where, in what countries, how, and in what form these rights are claimed to see that at times the question is actually the juridical question of rights, and at others it is the question of the assertion or claim of independence of the governed *vis-à-vis* governmentality (2008: 42).

Foucault argues that the history of liberalism in the west, from the eighteenth century on, moves between these two 'heterogeneous conceptions of freedom' (2008: 42). Both share the same liberal impulse, in that they aim to bring about and maintain the regulation and limitation of the power of government: the reference to heterogeneity does not imply that the two approaches are mutually exclusive. Nor is it a question of one approach consigning the other to irrelevance at any particular time or place; as Foucault writes, there is between them a 'ceaseless connection and a whole series of bridges, transits and joints' (2008: 43). However, and as recent history demonstrates, it is clear that the utilitarian approach is in the ascendency, and for Foucault this has been the case since the beginning of the nineteenth century, when 'the problem of utility' came to dominate over 'all the traditional problems of law' (2008: 44).

The reason of state and the phenomena of politics

It is at this point in (the text of) Foucault's lecture that he stops to consider what this change means for the reason of state, and to relate and exemplify how the aforementioned inflection of the reason of state by utilitarian liberalism plays itself out most profoundly. He suggests that this new and dominant liberal approach makes a bridge between the market as the site of exchange and truth, and government intervention dictated by the principal of utility, via the notion of 'interest'. From the eighteenth century onwards, the reason of state is no longer a self-referential process that begins and ends with the interest of the state and the maximisation of its resources; rather, government and the reason of state must account and make allowance for another set of subjects and identities. As Foucault explains it, previously the sovereign and/or the state were more or less co-substantial with regard to the things of the state: there was only one interest at stake because there was only one entity associated with, or having a hold over, everything that constituted or fell within the state. That singularity of interest is now pluralised. The reason of state no longer deals exclusively with (its own) things, but with 'the phenomena of politics' (2008: 45)—that is to say, it is required to negotiate with, and deal with disputes between, other imperatives, logics and wills.

In order to demonstrate this change, Foucault refers to the example of the penal system. He points out that in the seventeenth century any crime that was committed was seen to have been enacted against the power of the state: while murder or theft injured individuals, ultimately the real victim was sovereignty, and sovereignty responded to this injury by way of the 'spectacle of the scaffold', through torture and execution. In the eighteenth century, however, the public performance of the power of the sovereign, and the extreme forms of violence that accompanied it, is increasingly replaced by what Foucault refers to as 'the well-known principle of mildness of punishment' (2008: 46). This change is not the product of an increased sensitivity or human empathy, but rather of an economics. As Foucault writes, in this new regime punishment was to be calculated:

> in terms of the injured party's interests, in terms of redress for damage . . . Punishment will be rooted only in the play of interests of others, of the family circle, of society, and so on. Is it worthwhile punishing? What interest is there in punishing? What form must punishment take for it to be in society's interests to punish? Is there an interest in torturing, or is it more worthwhile to re-educate, and if so, how and up to what point? How much will it cost? The insertion of this thin phenomenal film of interest . . . as the only possible surface of government intervention, is what explains these changes, all of which must be referred back to the reorganization of governmental reason (2008: 46).

In the case of criminality, but also in a variety of other areas and socio-cultural fields (health, education, politics and what we would today call the field of the media, and even in a relatively autonomous field such as sport), the roles, attitudes and practices of government increasingly took on a liberal inflection, and were required to pay heed to what Foucault calls 'the fundamental question of liberalism . . . What is the utility value of government and all actions of government in a society where exchange determines the true value of things?' (2008: 46).

Europe as collective subject

Foucault goes on to argue that the ascendency of liberalism within Europe spread to and manifested itself in a wider, more global context; he provides an account of how, in the eighteenth century, Europe effectively comes into being—admittedly in an incipient and loose form—as an economic unit or subject, which then effectively takes the rest of the world as its object. He starts with mercantilism and what he calls the 'zero sum game', where competition for wealth between states presumes that the enrichment of some will necessarily involve the impoverishment of others (based on the notion that there is a limited supply of gold available). He suggests that this logic is superseded, in the middle of the eighteenth century, by this new strain of utilitarian liberalism championed by economists such as the physiocrats and Adam Smith, who argue that the freedom of the market does away with the zero sum game because, in its uninterrupted and unimpeded state, it necessarily increases wealth for everyone. Put simply, the idea is that pure competition leads to profit for both the buyer and the seller, and by extension the wider community. The idea of competition between European states increasing disparities of wealth is replaced by the notion of a Europe:

> of collective enrichment; Europe as a collective subject that, whatever the competition between states, or rather through

the competition between states, has to advance in the form of unlimited economic progress. The idea of progress, of a European progress, is a fundamental theme in liberalism . . . But if it is no longer to be a zero sum game . . . then it is necessary to summon round Europe, and for Europe, an increasingly extended market and even, if it comes to that, everything in the world can be put on the market (2008: 54–5).

This way of thinking about and dividing up the world—between what Foucault refers to as the players (Europe) and the stake (everything else) (2008: 55–6), is commensurate with European colonial expansion from the late eighteenth century to the present. Yet Foucault rejects the notion that it serves as the ideological basis for colonialism (already well underway by this time) or imperialism (which he suggests is not in place until the latter part of the nineteenth century). For Foucault, it is best characterised as a 'new form of global rationality, of a new calculation of the scale of the world' (2008: 56).

Foucault provides a number of useful examples of how this new global rationality is articulated and manifests itself. The first of these—and in many ways the most obvious—is to be found in the area of maritime law, and in particular the question of the sea being freely available for transit and traffic. The mid to late eighteenth century is a period when, as Armand Mattelart's work demonstrates (1994, 2000, 2003), the issue of networks and paths of communication was becoming of paramount importance; there is agreement between writers as different in their politics as Adam Smith, Kant and Voltaire that progress itself is to be equated with, facilitated by and predicated upon freedom of movement and communication—not just of goods and services, but also of people and ideas. The sea is one site where the question of free circulation is of pressing concern—and of vociferous debate and struggle. Foucault refers, for instance, to the way in which the notion of piracy undergoes a particularly back-and-forth discursive life. It is not as if activities of a piratical kind had not been endemic for thousands of years; what is at stake in, and new to, this particular discursive game is the appearance and deployment of the term within a wider ideological and juridical climate. What had to be accomplished, via the process of a 'juridification of the world' (2008: 56), was the accommodation, designation and regulation of certain kinds of dubious activities (or alternatively, the exercising of freedoms) within the wider discursive frame of the market. One person's freedom of enterprise is just as easily rendered as another person's piracy, and governments frequently both encouraged and made use of, and worked to suppress, the same type of activities.

Another example to which Foucault refers is Kant's work, published towards the end of the eighteenth century (2008: 57), on the possibility of and conditions for 'perpetual peace'. In keeping with liberalism and the notion of the truth of the market, Kant finds the potential for peace in nature. Nature is characterised as intending the world to be given over to human activity—particularly production and exchange—which when translated into and guaranteed by law allows people to live in all corners and conditions of the world, effectively at peace with one another. In these terms, all forms of law (civil and international) are both derived from the conditions and truth of nature, and carry out the intentions and dispositions of nature to populate the world. As Foucault writes, 'Perpetual peace . . . is manifested . . . in the commercial relations stretching across the whole world. The guarantee of perpetual peace is therefore actually commercial globalization' (2008: 58).

Freedom and security

Foucault suggests that this recourse to, and dependence upon, naturalism in liberal thought is central to the way that it configures the relation between governmentality and the reason of state on the one hand, and the notion of freedom on the other. From the perspective of Adam Smith and the physiocrats, for instance, freedom is not to be equated or confused with the idea of human rights or individual liberties. The lesson that liberal economists draw from nature is not that 'people must be given the freedom to act as they wish', or that 'governments must be as little authoritarian as possible' (2008: 61). Rather, they deduce that government must know the spontaneous and natural mechanisms, rhythms and movements of the market, and:

> Once it knows these mechanisms, it must . . . undertake to respect them. But it does not mean that it provides itself with a juridical framework respecting . . . the basic rights of individuals. It means . . . that it arms its politics with a precise, continuous, clear and distinct knowledge of what is taking place in society, in the market, and in the economic circuits, so that the limitation of its power is not given by respect for the freedom of individuals, but simply by the evidence of economic analysis . . . It is limited by evidence (2008: 61–2).

It is within the confines of empiricism that the liberal-inflected reason of state is faced with the requirement to produce the conditions of freedom—or, as Foucault writes, 'I am going to see to it that you are free to be free' (2008: 63)—but at the centre of this process is the dilemma that the conditions of freedom can only be brought about and maintained via recourse to apparatuses, mechanisms, policies and practices of government intervention.

The reason for this dilemma, as Foucault explains it, is that there is a cost associated with the continued production of freedom, and that 'principle of calculation is what is called security' (2008: 65). To understand this situation, we need to return to the question of the play of interests—of interest in the plural. The reason of state is always required to relate interest to interest, and to weigh up and consider whether the intervention that facilitates the advance of one form of interest might constitute a danger to the interest of another party. The most obvious context for this pull of interests is when the interest of an individual or small group conflicts with and threatens the collective interest; however, what is clearly the most dangerous situation is when the interest of one party threatens the wider operations and mechanisms of the freedom of the market. The example to which Foucault refers involves the potential conflict of interests between the owners of the means of production. In the first instance, the government must ensure that the natural relation between the supply of and demand for labour produces a price that suits the interests of both groups. However, it also must ensure that one group does not achieve a position of power or advantage that would seriously distort the balance of interests, because this would constitute a collective danger. This could occur if by means of the threat of strikes workers managed to inflate wages artificially; or if producers were able to force the enactment of legislation that allowed them to ignore their responsibilities regarding the health and safety of their workers.

Foucault identifies three main consequences that arise from this necessity of navigating between freedom and security. The first of these is that the liberalism-inflected reason of state is identified with the motto 'Live dangerously' (2008: 66). The everyday is transformed into a world of potential dangers, calamities, losses and injuries that are quite different in kind from the apocalyptic scenarios and sensibilities of the Middle Ages. Foucault writes of a 'political culture of danger in the nineteenth century' (2008: 66) that gives rise to campaigns concerning health and hygiene, and fears about sexual perversion, moral corruption and racial degeneration, and he refers to the sudden rise in the popularity of detective fiction as another symptom of this culture. We can think of Sherlock Holmes being forced to deal not just with the criminal genius of Moriarty, but with an endless number of more quotidian criminals—the scientist corrupted by his too-zealous pursuit of knowledge, or the bastard son who attempts to murder his half-brother in order to gain the familial inheritance. These figures stand as an example of the perennial danger of talented members of the upper or professional classes turning their intellects and resources against the law, and society in general. This tendency is evidenced by the rise and prominence of the insurance industry, where vicissitudes, setbacks and disasters are presumed and integrated into the economics of business and the everyday. Taken to its logical extension, it produces the possibility—recently outlined and then quickly abandoned by the Pentagon—of an insurance market 'in terrorism', whereby investors could invest in and against the possibility of wars, bombings, assassinations and other human crimes and atrocities.

The second consequence of liberalism, commensurate with and tied to this culture of danger, is the proliferation of mechanisms and procedures 'of control, constraint, and coercion' (2008: 67) and, above all else, surveillance. Foucault refers to Bentham's proposition that the panopticon 'is the very formula of liberal government' (2008: 67) because it allows for the widest, most constant and effective overseeing of conduct; the most rigorous collection of relevant data; and therefore the most accurate and reliable evaluation of when intervention might be required.

The third consequence of liberalism is an imperative to continue to produce new freedoms and animate dormant ones via the introduction of new mechanisms and instances of government control and regulation. The example Foucault uses here is the US 'New Deal' of the 1930s, where Roosevelt—faced with a crisis that threatened to overturn the dominance of capitalism—was forced to employ measures that produced freedoms (to work, to spend, to unionise) that conflicted with the liberal belief in the truth and autonomy of the market (and were condemned as threatening freedom).

These three consequences, when taken together, constitute what Foucault refers to as the 'crisis of governmentality' (2008: 68), and by extension the 'crisis of liberalism' (2008: 69); put simply, the attempt on the part of liberal government to intervene in order to protect, produce and guarantee freedoms 'risk producing exactly the opposite' (2008: 69). This has been most apparent when governments have attempted to fight off the threats posed by revolutionary forces—National Socialism, fascism, communism and extreme nationalism. For liberal economic theorists, the question is whether the means employed to deal with revolutionary forces do not in themselves pose an equal threat to freedom. Foucault writes that:

> around Keynes, around the economic interventionist policy perfected between 1930 and 1960, immediately before and after the war, all these interventions . . . brought about what we can call a crisis of liberalism, and this crisis manifests itself in a number of re-evaluations, re-appraisals, and new projects in the art of government which were formulated immediately before and after the war in Germany, and which are presently being formulated in America (2008: 69).

Neo-liberalism

The first half of *The Birth of Biopolitics* provides an account of the development of the relation between liberalism and the reason of state, from the seventeenth century up to the Depression, Keynesian economics and Roosevelt's New Deal. The second half of the book is devoted to Foucault's extension of his narrative to take in the most recent manifestations of this relation, specifically its inflection by German and American neo-liberal theories, which have become more or less a form of doxa for governments in the west since the 1980s.

As with the opening lecture/chapter on liberalism, Foucault commences the section on neo-liberalism with a reported quote, this time from the US art critic Bernard Berenson. Foucault writes that:

> He was almost one hundred years old, approaching death, when he said something like: 'God knows I fear the destruction of the world by the atomic bomb, but there is at least one

thing I fear as much, and that is the invasion of humanity by the state.' I think this is the purest, clearest expression of a state-phobia one of the most constant features of which is its coupling with fear of the atomic bomb (2008: 76).

Foucault links the rise of neo-liberalism to the increase in government intervention in the economy as a result of the Depression and World War II, but also more generally to the political crises of the first part of the twentieth century. These include the instability and hyperinflation of the Weimar Republic, the disastrous 'planned economies' of the Soviet Union, and the rise of fascism in Germany, Italy, Austria and elsewhere. Foucault identifies these examples, along with the vicissitudes of post-war planning in Britain (2008: 76), as catalysts for the development of what he refers to as a 'phobia of the state' (2008: 75).

Foucault commences his discussion of German neo-liberalism by way of reference to the situation in Europe in 1948, where a number of countries—Germany, Austria, Italy and Belgium—were dealing with three major post-war imperatives: first, there was reconstruction, which involved both the reestablishment of a peacetime economy and the integration of significant new developments—social, technological and politico-geographic; second, reconstruction needed to be commensurate with and accommodate the dictates of American influence and the Marshall Plan; and third, there was a need for the development of social and political policies designed to close off the possibility of the re-emergence of fascism and Nazism.

These objectives were not to be met by taking the Keynesian path; for both German and America neo-liberals, the British economist Keynes, with his insistence on the role of state planning and the controlled economy, was 'the main doctrinal adversary . . . the common enemy' (2008: 79). Instead, they would be brought about through the imposition of a limitation on the role of the state with regard to the economy. Foucault traces this institutional and discursive trajectory in Germany, starting in 1948 with administrative committee reports recommending the abolition of price controls and 'the immediate deregulation' (2008: 80) of the economy, and a speech by the influential liberal bureaucrat (and future chancellor) Ludwig Erhard, to the effect that the state must renounce economic intervention on the grounds that 'only a state that establishes both the freedom and responsibility of citizens can legitimately speak in the name of the people' (2008: 81).

Foucault reads Erhard's pronouncement in two ways. On the one hand, it is referring to Germany's Nazi past, and making the point that any government that violates the rights and freedoms of its citizens, and turns the laws of the state into a mechanism for doing violence to the people, is not representative. The idea here is to effect a separation of the Nazi regime and its atrocities from the German people: what was done by Hitler was not done in their name, because the Nazi juridical and bureaucratic framework was not derived from, or sanctioned by, any legitimate authority. For Foucault, however, the more significant reading follows from this discursive production of the Third Reich as a socio-political vacuum. In effect, Erhard is claiming that:

> in the current state of affairs . . . it is clearly not possible to lay claim to the historical rights for a . . . still to be reconstituted German state, when these rights are debarred by history itself. It is not possible to claim juridical legitimacy insomuch as no apparatus, no consensus, and no collective will can manifest itself in a situation in which Germany is . . . divided . . . and . . . occupied. So there are no historical rights, there is no juridical legitimacy, on which to found a new German state (2008: 82).

The mechanism that will serve to found and guarantee the new German state is the market. The freedoms that are created in and through the market, and the economic growth and development (and material prosperity) that accompanies it, will work to produce political sovereignty. This is because 'the economic game of freedom' will produce 'a permanent consensus of . . . agents within these economic processes, as investors, workers, employers, and trade unions' (2008: 84).

With regard to the semiotic significance of the economic *vis-à-vis* the wider socio-cultural field, Foucault makes a comparison between sixteenth and twentieth century Germany. He refers to Max Weber's argument that in the sixteenth century wealth was often read as a sign from God—of election, of righteousness, of the fact of impending salvation. In the twentieth century, signs of wealth or economic prosperity—such as a strong balance of payments surplus, growth in GDP, a strong and stable currency, high wages and low debt—signify the consensus of the state and something more—the founding and election of the German state based on a principle of economic freedom, which is pointedly different from Germany's history of territorial aggression.

Foucault argues that this is a radical departure for liberalism, which from the sixteenth century on had both presumed the (reason of) state and attempted to limit its powers of intervention. Faced with the unlimited growth of state power under the Nazis, German liberalism simply replaces the state with the free market, which brings the political into being and allows Germany to assert itself without arousing the suspicion of its European neighbours. This is achieved by drawing all the main socio-political organisations—capitalist institutions, political parties, the Catholic Church, trade unions—into the 'game of freedom' as committed players. Even those institutions with a strong antipathy to or suspicion of capitalism, such as the trade unions and the Social Democrats, must come to accept that 'in neo-liberalism there was the finally fulfilled promise of a middle way or third order between capitalism and socialism' (2008: 88). In this way the market takes up, in a naturalised way, a position as both the arbiter of value and a guarantor against the state overreaching itself.

The Freiburg School

The ideological ground of German neo-liberalism is to be found in the work of Erhard and the economists of the Freiburg School (who included William Ropke, Walter Eucken, Franz Blom and the Austrian Friedrich von Hayek). Foucault makes an interesting comparison between that group and the Frankfurt School, which parallel each other in terms of 'their dates and equally their fate' (2008: 105): members of both groups were forced into exile during the Nazi period. The more interesting connection, however, is of a theoretical nature: Foucault suggests that both schools take as their starting point Max Weber's problematisation of 'the irrational rationality of capitalist society' (2008: 105); their approaches to this problem, however, are quite different. For the Frankfurt School, the problem was how to develop a rational socio-cultural sensibility that would mitigate the worst features of capitalism, while for the Freiburg School the point was to rediscover the conditions that facilitated the truth and rationality of the market, as opposed to the irrationality of capitalist practices and government intervention.

Both forms of irrationality weighed heavily upon neo-liberal thought in post-war Germany, enough for Foucault to suggest that 'Nazism was, in a way, the epistemological and political "road to Damascus" for the Freiburg School' (2008: 106). He argues, however, that the experience of the Weimar Republic, coupled with the rise of Nazism, did not constitute a completely new set of problems for neo-liberal theory. He provides a detailed account of the various social, political, cultural and ideological contexts, dating from the middle of the nineteenth century, that for neo-liberal thought necessarily culminated in something like Nazism. The four contexts can be described, very generally, as a belief that liberal economics was incompatible with (German) nationalism; the doxa that state socialism was a requisite part of maintaining national unity; the centralisation of economic planning brought about by military aggression or conditions of war; and the rise of the welfare state.

What Foucault refers to as the *'coup de force* of the German neo-liberals'* is the refusal to categorise or consider the Nazi economic regime as anomalous or arbitrary; instead, Nazism demonstrates that:

> these four elements which German economic and political history successively brought onto the scene of government action are economically linked to each other and if you adopt one of them you will not escape the other three (2008: 110).

For Ropke, Keynesian interventionism was linked to Nazism and the Soviet planned economy by way of its anti-liberal logic. This seems in one sense a difficult position to maintain, since with Nazism (and indeed, Soviet communism) the state apparently 'withers away', being replaced by the party understood as a manifestation of the people (or with the Soviet Union, of a class). However, for Ropke Nazism is understood as the culmination of both state interventionism and anti-capitalist communism. Nazism, rather than doing away with the state, requires and constitutes an intensification and proliferation of the state, which now makes its way into every corner of life. Ropek also argues that the anti-liberalism of the British post-war government and the American New Deal led 'to the Goring plan, to the four-year plan of 1936' (2008: 110–11), since they were all driven by the imperative for this new kind of state 'to extend beyond itself' (2008: 112). Even the notion that Nazism grows out of, and is a kind of critical response to, the excesses of capitalist alienation is turned against itself. Nazism is configured as the supreme form of alienation, of the people simultaneously driven to a fever of ecstasy and narcotised by Nuremburg and the Volkswagen; and, 'These mass phenomena of standardization and the spectacle are linked to statism, anti-liberalism, and not a market economy' (2008: 114). Every defect of market-driven capitalism, then, can be understood as a defect of the (excesses of the) state; and the only access we have to rationality, pace the Frankfurt School, is via the market. Foucault makes the point that, for the Freiburg School, the idea/ideal of competition no longer serves as a form of natural truth:

> It is absolutely not a given of nature. The game, mechanisms, and the effect of competition which we identify and enhance . . . [are] not the result of a natural interplay of appetites, instincts, behavior, and so on . . . The beneficial effects of competition . . . are due to a formal privilege . . . Competition is a principle of formalization. Competition has an internal logic; it has its own structure. Its effects are only produced if this logic is respected . . . Competition is therefore an historical object of governmental art (2008: 120).

The art of government, from this perspective, is defined by its adherence and resemblance, and consistency with regard, to market competition, while at the same time being marked by an acceptance of the need for intervention, vigilance and suspicion.

Foucault refers to areas that exemplify how the pragmatics of neo-liberalism sought to deal with the vexed relation between government economic policy and intervention, the market and the principle of competition. The first of these is the problem of monopolies. In classical liberal economic theory, monopolies are seen as more or less inevitable, an aspect of market competition that, from time to time, requires some form of government intervention. For the German neo-liberals, however, monopolies are seen as an archaic feature incommensurate with modern market competition (a historical consequence derived, for instance, from the medieval practice of the Crown bestowing a monopoly in one service or trade); or else they are a consequence of unsound state intervention. Neo-liberal theory argues, for instance, that juridical contexts and practices (with regard, say, to patent rights or company law) historically have facilitated monopolistic dispositions and tendencies—inadvertently or otherwise. Another obvious example is protectionist policies, which are often employed, *de facto*, to encourage or protect homegrown monopolies because the socio-political consequences (mass unemployment, alienating or antagonising powerful political lobby groups, undermining attempts to assuage or woo particular demographics) are not palatable. When monopolies do arise more or less naturally, the neo-liberal argument is that they are either an aberration that would be swept aside by their own removal from a connection to the competitive ethos (the monopolistic tendency would be conservative, disposing them away from technical innovation, thus facilitating their eventual decline or demise), or that the inflation of the monopolistic price would encourage competitors, thus forcing the monopolistic price down to a competitive level. In both cases, monopolies fall victim to their own alienation from the principle of competition.

The second area dealt with by Foucault is what he calls 'the question of conformable action' (2008: 137), whereby the government is required to intervene in the economy at either a regulatory or an organisational level. Foucault analyses two influential texts on the principles of economic policy, both authored by the Freiburg School's Walter Euback and published in the 1950s (2008: 138). Euback argues that the primary focus of intervention must be to maintain price stability, even at the expense of other factors such as the maintenance of purchasing power or full employment. This does not entail price fixing, but rather the control of inflation, which facilitates the reduction of costs and thus works to maintain or encourage competition between businesses. This is where the conflict between persevering with economic principles and giving way to (misguided) socio-political pressures is most fraught: Euback warns, for instance, against the policy of intervening to reduce unemployment because this is something that the maintenance of price stability will fix, naturally, over time. This requires, however, a complete renunciation of humanist discourses and sensibilities. For the Freiburg School, the situation and experience of unemployment needed to be abstracted and configured as a formal entity. As Ropek explains, 'what is an unemployed person?

He is not suffering from an economic disability; he is not a social victim. He is a worker in transit . . . between an unprofitable activity and a . . . profitable activity' (2008: 139).

This tendency to abstract and formalise socio-political issues (Foucault points out that Euback's father was a distinguished Kantian scholar) is also meant to inform the 'organisational actions' of government. The term refers to those sectors that constitute the framework of the market: framework is here understood as an all encompassing notion, taking in any and all groups, identities, institutions, contexts and factors (populations, the law, trade unions, the climate, resources, technology, infrastructure) that might bear upon or contribute to the workings of the market. Euback takes up the history of government agricultural policy in Germany and Europe, and shows that for a variety of political reasons, agriculture has never truly been integrated into the market economy. (In one of the lighter moments that distinguish the lectures from his tomes, Foucault comments, 'This text is from 1952' (2008: 140), which indicates the longevity of the issue.) What does the government need to do to intervene with regard to the framework? On the one hand, there is the question of what we might call 'value adding' at a material level; this involves providing appropriate training to workers, ensuring that technology is up to date, and helping with decision-making by providing relevant scientific information. On the other hand, once we get into the socio-cultural sphere, the discourse again becomes entirely formalistic: workers will be relocated by 'enabling population transfers . . . [and] migration' (2008: 140); laws will need to be introduced and changed in order to free up ownership, change patterns of inheritance, and weaken entrenched institutions and practices of conservatism; and finally, the allocation and methods of exploitation of the soil will be predicated, not on tradition or socio-cultural preference, but in terms of the principles of the competitive ethos.

The third area that required government intervention, according to the Freiburg School, was social policy. In this regard, it sets itself against the principles and tendencies of the 'welfare states' of the US New Deal and the post-war British planned state. The social policy of the welfare state is characterised, very generally, as working towards 'the objective of everyone having relatively equal access to consumer goods' (2008: 142). It pursues this objective by way of three main methods: it restrains economic activity that might produce inequality or social disruption (such as the privatisation of education or health care); it socialises some socially and politically sensitive areas of consumption (heat, water, transport), and intervenes to redistribute resources (by introducing family allowances, tax concessions and scholarships to students from poor families); and finally, economic growth is met with a concomitant increase in the spread and generosity of welfare policy.

Welfare state policy is totally incompatible with neo-liberal social policy—indeed, economic inequality is a requirement and a consequence of competition and the maintenance of price stability. The only redistribution of resources allowed within such a system would be a minimal reallocation from top to bottom on purely pragmatic grounds—death removes potential workers and consumers from the equation, so the population needs to be kept healthy. Similarly, there is no place for socialisation within a neo-liberal framework. Risk to the individual or group (of health, unemployment, damage) will not be guaranteed by the state, but through the operations of the competitive market: the privatisation of risk provides individuals with the means or the opportunity to protect themselves. Foucault writes that these responses to the principles of the welfare state lead to the conclusion that, for neo-liberalism:

> there is only one true and fundamental social policy: economic growth. The fundamental form of social policy must not be something that works against economic policy and compensates for it; social policy must not follow strong economic growth by becoming more generous. Economic growth and

only economic growth should enable all individuals to achieve a level of income that will allow them the individual insurances, access to private property, and individual or familial capitalization with which to absorb risks (2008: 144).

This economic 'formalisation' of the social and of social relations is one of the two significant ways in which neo-liberal theory (and, in the new West German Republic, practice) addresses the issue of government; the second is via the proposed utilisation of the juridical frames and apparatuses of the state. Foucault refers to a symposium that took place in 1939, organised by the French epistemologist Louis Rougier, which brought together all the ideologues of the different branches of neo-liberalism, principally the Freiburg School and Hayek and von Mises; the latter two would be intermediaries between the Freiburg School and 'American neo-liberalism which gives rise to the anarcho-liberalism of the Chicago school, Milton Friedman etcetera' (2008: 161). In his introduction to the symposium, Rougier makes four points with regard to the relation between neo-liberal imperatives and the legal field: first, he emphasises that the market, while operating as a form and manifestation of natural law, is always closely tied to, dependent upon, and inflected by a 'juridical framework' (2008: 161); second, he argues that contemporary legal institutions, legislature and practices are not necessarily best suited to 'safeguarding the freedom of transactions' (2008: 161); third, he suggests that this area of study has been neglected by economists, and needs to be brought to the forefront of theoretical consideration; and fourth, he maintains that, 'To be liberal . . . is to be essentially progressive in the sense of a constant adaptation of the legal order to scientific discoveries . . . [and] to the progress of economic organization and technique' (2008: 161–2).

Foucault suggests that while there are aspects of Rougier's introduction that would clearly be unacceptable or contrary to neo-liberalism (the old liberal notion of the market being derived from a natural order, for instance), on the whole it articulates and accurately represents the neo-liberal position with regard to the place and role of the legal system. This position is that the law does not simply reflect economic laws, but rather is part of an ensemble of activities, rules, dispositions and discourses that comprise and constitute a wider system. Further, each part of this wider system (comprising such diverse elements as the law, capitalism, culture and politics) is tied in with, and inflected by, the others. What this means, for instance, is that capitalism has a history (for instance, the trajectory of its relation to the state) which is constitutive of capitalism (various fields and forces inflect and even transform capitalism). Foucault argues that the theoretical and political dimension to this move is largely to rebut the Marxist notion of capitalism as a thing of and for itself. If the fate of capitalism is only subject to its own logics, then 'the end of capitalism is revealed in the historical impasses it is currently manifesting' (2008: 165). On the other hand, if capitalism is both a thing in itself and a series of historical possibilities and forms of transformation waiting to happen, part of a wider unfolding system, then the contemporary crisis of capitalism is of a temporary nature.

For the neo-liberals, what offers up the possibility for the recrafting (and eventually the transformation) of contemporary capitalism is the rule of law. Their notion of the rule of law is derived from eighteenth-century German legal history, and it is primarily defined by what it is opposed to—both despotism (the sovereign's will determines the law) and the police state (the law is coterminous and continuous with regard to public authorities and the apparatuses of the reason of state). This rule of law is characterised by specific mechanisms, relations and processes, but only insofar as they deny or interrupt despotism and the police state; in short, the rule of law necessarily operates as a 'judicial arbitration between individuals and the public authorities' (2008: 170).

How was this to happen with regard to the market? Foucault refers to Hayek's dictum, in *The Constitution of Liberty*, that the state's legal intervention in the economic sphere should only 'take the form . . . of formal economic legislation' (2008: 171). For Hayek, this meant the opposite—not only to the excesses of Nazism and to Keynesian state intervention, but also to any legal imposition of a planned economy. The rule of law will:

> have the possibility of formulating certain measures of a general kind, but these must remain completely formal and must never pursue a particular end. It must not tell people what they must and must not do; it must not be inscribed within an overall economic choice (2008: 172).

Legal intervention in the economy must be made on the basis of principle rather than desired effect, it must allow agents their own (legally inflected) decisions and it must be applied fairly and consistently across the socio-political sphere—which includes the state and its apparatuses and institutions. An example of this last point can be found in the attempts by neo-liberal governments in the west, in the 1980s and 1990s, to apply competitive policies to social utilities and services, including the area of education. What this meant was that state institutions (schools, universities) were perceived to be operating in a context and manner that worked against competition, because they had access to state funding and other resources (buildings, infrastructure) that were denied to potential private suppliers. The idea was that every potential supplier of educational services could operate on a level playing field, so in theory a prestigious traditional state university could find itself outbid for its lecture theatres, academics, students and halls of residence by a company that had no history of involvement in, or ethical commitment to, the field of education.

American neo-liberalism

Foucault argues that this version of neo-liberalism, committed to a rule of law that worked to guarantee the rule of pure market competition across the wider socio-cultural sphere, more or less produced the modern German state and helped influence governmental policy in Europe and America. Foucault notes that in the United States the contexts and factors that influenced the development of neo-liberalism mirrored the situation in Europe, while being characterised by specifically local inflections. The Roosevelt New Deal was succeeded and accentuated by the 'projects of economic and social interventionism developed during the war' (2008: 216), and by the various forms of state intervention (in areas such as education, race and poverty) during the post-war/pre-Nixon administrations, particularly in the period of the Johnson presidency. While this level of state intervention was not as marked as in the United Kingdom, for example, it still acted as the catalyst for, and 'formed the adversary and target' of, neo-liberal thought; this history of state intervention was what 'it was constructed against or which it opposed in order to form itself and develop' (2008: 217).

Foucault identifies three other factors as being largely specific to the US context. First, he suggests that whereas in the eighteenth century European liberalism functioned as a 'moderating principle' (2008: 217) with regard to the reason of state, in the United States liberalism is the position from which the state comes into being—that is, the American War of Independence can be said to have been a war fought against the state (Imperial Britain), which came to constitute the point of legitimation for the type of state that would form the newly independent United States of America. The state had forfeited its historical rights, and in this historical vacuum 'the demands for liberalism found the state' (2008: 217). Second, and concomitantly, he makes the point that whereas in European history—from the eighteenth century on—liberalism is present as an ideological player in a wide range of contentious issues (nationalism, imperialism, the right of law), in the United States liberalism is the only ideology brought to bear on important questions such as slavery, protectionism and states' rights. Third, and finally, in the United States interventionist policies are opposed by an unholy alliance of right- and left-wing political factions: from the right state intervention is identified as being socialist, and therefore threatening, while on the left it is associated—particularly during the Johnson administration—with imperialism and the build-up of US militarism.

The distinction between European and American liberalism, then, can be characterised as the difference between a strong but specific set of practices, inclinations, dispositions and choices on the one hand, and a general 'mode of thought, analysis and imagination', a 'grid of sociological and historical decipherment' (2008: 219) on the other. Foucault refers to two areas that demonstrate the workings of this liberal imaginary. The first of these is the issue of human capital. He suggests that for neo-liberal theorists (he refers particularly to the work of Theodore Schultz and Gary Becker), the analysis of labour within classical economic theory has suffered from being abstracted. The task is to move from a position where human capital is simply quantified (and hence misrecognised) as one factor within consideration of the relation between production, exchange and consumption, to a theory of labour that both places it at the centre of economic activity, and understands it as a series of 'substitutable choices' (2008: 222). There is a change in emphasis here, away from economics as process and towards a notion of practice, of practicalities:

> To bring labour into the field of economic analysis, we must put ourselves in the position of the person who works . . . What does working mean for the person who works? What system of choice and rationality does the activity of work conform to? As a result, on the basis of this grid which projects a principle of strategic rationality on the activity of work, we will be able to see in what respects and how the qualitative differences of work may have an economic type of effect (2008: 223).

The next step in this process of neo-liberal reasoning is the principle that people work 'in order to earn a wage', with a wage being defined as 'the product or return on a capital' (2008: 224). We are here moving away, as Foucault points out, from the notion that the worker is someone who receives an income from time to time; instead, the worker is understood as being temporal and mechanistic, as a machine that 'has a lifespan, a length of time in which it can be used, and obsolescence, and an aging' (2008: 224–5). This human machine is an ensemble of things—first and foremost a commodity, but also an entrepreneur and a producer with regard to the self as commodity.

What differentiates these human commodities, and how are they constituted? They are made up of innate elements (hereditary features) and any factors that produce what we could call 'improvements'— such as education, parenting, health care, acquiring skills, experience and physical development. Genetic advantages, and the various forms of investment (from being fed well and having access to education to receiving parental love and attention) likely to produce improvements, then, are the two factors that go into differentiating and evaluating the human commodity. Now, while it is not yet respectable or even possible to discuss, in a politically palatable form, the issue of genetic engineering as a branch of economics, or as an aspect of socio-economic policy (limiting the number of children of couples with genetic dispositions towards certain diseases, for instance), neo-liberal theory has looked at how the value-added dimension of human capital can both explain the rise of economies devastated by the war (Germany, Japan) and be used to guide and determine investment in human capital with developing countries. In all spheres of life, neo-liberalism takes what is effectively an economic cost-benefit, and applies it to and uses it to scrutinise and test:

> governmental action, gauge its validity, and to object to activi-
> ties of the public authorities on the grounds of their abuses,
> excesses, futility, and wasteful expenditure. In short, the eco-
> nomic grid is not applied . . . in order to understand social
> processes and make them intelligible . . . it involves criticism

of the governmentality actually exercised which is not just a political or juridical criticism; it is a market criticism, the cynicism of a market criticism opposed to the action of public authorities (2008: 246).

Foucault argues that this same regime of logic is deployed in the neo-liberal analysis of, and attitude towards, criminality and the penal system—a disposition he traces back to liberal penal reform and ideology of the eighteenth century (and the work of Bentham and Beccaria). Referring to Gary Becker's work, Foucault shows how neo-liberalism reformulates crime as a form of economic risk, or even speculation: criminality is emptied of any moral, psychological or anthropological discourse. Instead, crime is framed (much as with the issue of human capital) as something in which the subject, the neo-liberal commodity as entrepreneur, might invest. If a person commits a criminal act (murder, robbery, fraud, rape or possessing an illegal drug), they are simply investing their capital while taking into account the concomitant risk attached, as with any other commercial venture. One of the consequences of this move is that it removes the binary, present since the eighteenth century, of crime/criminal. For Foucault, the influence of the human sciences resulted in the two being separated out—so, for instance, a variety of psychological factors had to be considered in determining the guilt of, and by extension the appropriate punishment for, the person committing a crime. With neo-liberalism, however, the two are conflated within a logic determined by the relation between supply, demand, profit and risk. Foucault writes that 'economic behavior is the grid of intelligibility one will adopt on the behavior of a new individual' (2008: 252); it becomes 'the surface of contact between the individual and power exercised on him' (2008: 252–3). The 'regulation of power over the individual' (2008: 253) is to be formulated out of the notion and category of the human as an economic ensemble.

Much the same logic applies when the crime/criminal is considered from the perspective of the juridical field; as Foucault puts it, 'The penal system . . . will have to react to the supply of crime' (2008: 253). Punishment is now considered from a position comparable to that formulated by Bentham and Beccaria in the eighteenth century, where crime is punished because it infringes upon the domain of others, and does harm; to use Becker's term, it produces 'negative externalities' (2008: 253). The level of punishment should be of a scale that will dispose individuals to refrain from taking on the risk involved; murder may be profitable, but the risk associated with it is severe. However, the neo-liberal position differs from eighteenth century liberalism with regard to what Foucault calls the level of its 'law enforcement' (2008: 254), which he describes as:

> the set of instruments employed to give social and political reality to the act of prohibition . . . It will be the quantity of punishment . . . It will be size, activity, zeal, and competence of the apparatuses responsible for detecting crimes . . . It will be how quickly judges make their judgments, and how severe they are within the margins the law leaves them. It will be . . . the degree to which the penalty applied can be modified, lessened, or possibly increased by the prison administration . . . Law enforcement is the set of instruments of action which, on the market for crime, opposes a negative demand to the supply of crime (2008: 254–5).

Despite the intensity of force brought to bear on the criminal (by the state, the judiciary, the police, and even to some extent external players such political parties and the media), neo-liberalism undertakes to play for lesser stakes than Bentham, whose panopticon was meant, in theory, to bring about the disappearance of crime. The scope of the neo-liberal juridical agenda is more limited: from a purely economic perspective, there is little point in trying to eradicate all crime—or indeed, in reducing certain types of crime—because the level of expenditure required (the cost) would be considerably in excess of the result (the benefit). For Becker and the neo-liberals, there are only two questions with regard to the law and crime: 'How many offences should be permitted? Second, how many offenders should go unpunished?' (2008: 256).

Conclusion

The rise of a specific neo-liberal relation and sensibility with regard to both the human subject and the criminal (and by extension, every category of problematical subjectivity developed through the power–knowledge nexus, including the insane and the sexual pervert) has influenced and inflected both the reason of state and the disciplinary logics and mechanisms (and the various forms of the exercising of power) that accompany it. More specifically, it has introduced a significant new dimension to the operations and imperatives of biopower; at the very least, if the anthropological or psychological subject has been supplanted by an economic subject, then:

> what appears on the horizon of this kind of analysis is not . . . the project of an exhaustively disciplinary society in which the legal network hemming in individuals is taken over and extended, internally, by . . . normative mechanisms. Nor is it a society in which a mechanism of general normalization and the exclusion of those who cannot be normalized is needed. On the horizon of this analysis we see instead the image . . . or theme-program of a society in which there is the optimization of systems of difference, in which minority individuals and practices are tolerated, in which action is brought to bear on the rules of the game rather than on the players, and finally in which there is an environmental type of intervention instead of the internal subjugation of individuals (2008: 259–60).

This ongoing relationship between the workings of power, discursive regimes and the mechanisms and apparatuses of biopower and normalisation on the one hand, and the production, negotiation and crafting of different modes and forms of subjectivity on the other, has been a central theme in Foucault's work. In our next chapter, we will provide an account of what we could call Foucault's genealogy of the subject, and consider how different regimes and games of truth dispose and delimit, and simultaneously produce a certain flexibility and freedom, with regard to what Foucault terms 'technologies of the self' (1985, 1986a).

5
~

Subjectivity and technologies of the self

Introduction

Foucault has written widely about the processes and techniques involved in the production of subjects—most particularly in *Discipline and Punishment* and *The History of Sexuality*, but also in various lecture series collected in books, such as *Abnormal* (2003a), *Security, Territory, Population* (2007a) and *The Birth of Biopolitics* (2008). He characterises this work, however, as part of a wider project of 'constructing a history of what we have done and, at the same time, a diagnosis of what we are' (2007a: 152). This analysis of 'the genealogy of the subject in Western civilization . . . has to take into account not just techniques of domination but also techniques of the self' (2007a: 154). The first volume of *The History of Sexuality* clearly falls into the former category, but it also presages the trajectory of the subsequent two volumes, and their concern with the subject's relation to the self.

The terms 'subject' and 'subjectivity' are critical to an understanding of Foucault's oeuvre: the objective of his work, he states, 'has been to create a history of the different modes by which, in our culture, human beings are made subjects' (Foucault 1985: 7). In this chapter, we turn our attention to what Foucault means by 'subjectivity', and the terms and contexts he posits for the practices of being/becoming a subject.

Historicising the subject

Foucault's perspective is built on his long investigation and analysis of western philosophy from Ancient Greek times to the present. Throughout his writing, he keeps coming back to the subject of the subject: from his early works such as *The Order of Things* where he examines how, in particular historical moments, people become objects of knowledge, through to the last two volumes of *The History of Sexuality*, where he examines how people constitute themselves as discursive entities within the limits imposed by time, place and regimes of power. Throughout, his work deals with the emergence of what he calls 'man' in history and in discourse. By analysing the many different understandings of the subject that exist, Foucault shows that the subject takes on different forms in different historical periods. Consequently, Foucault suggests, no individual should be understood to be inherently or intrinsically him or herself. We become subjects as a result of the various networks of relationships and discourses in which we grow up and live. As Foucault writes in the first volume of *The History of Sexuality*:

> confronted by a power that is law, the subject who is constituted as subject—who is 'subjected'—is he who obeys. To the formal homogeneity of power in these various instances corresponds the general form of submission in the one who is constrained by it (1978: 85).

It is not simply that the subject is one who is subject to legal obligations, as legal theory suggests; rather, the subject is the one who actually submits to, and is recognisable in terms of, those obligations. Foucault argues strongly against the naturalist view of the self that comes out of readings of Rousseau's work, and presents the obverse view: that it is not the individual who emerges first and power that then comes along to break our spirits; rather, subjects become individuals precisely because of power. Power, manifested particularly through discourses of truth and knowledge, makes us what we are. Human beings-as-subjects are therefore contingent, rather than innate or natural.

Genealogy of desire

In Volume 1 of *The History of Sexuality*, Foucault argues that, in the west, sexuality comes to assume the role of a constant, something outside and beyond historical inflection or transformation, and as such a privileged site where the truth of the subject can be identified. The main argument is that it is only via the authority of certain fields and discourses of scientific knowledge (most obviously, but not exclusively, health and psychology), intertwined with the more general operations of disciplinary power, that subjects come to recognise themselves as objects of repression who have been separated off from knowledge of themselves. From this perspective, the imperative to 'know thyself' is to be translated as 'know thy desires'.

For Foucault, this notion of the centrality (and universality) of the desiring subject has a rather strange aspect to it, in that it is taken up and affirmed not only by traditional bodies of theory (psychiatry, conventional psychoanalysis), but also by those theories and theorists that set themselves apart from, or are opposed to, conventional theory. He is referring to the development whereby both Jacques Lacan (in his critique of institutionalised psychoanalysis) and Gilles Deleuze and Felix Guattari (in their trenchantly anti-Oedipal *Anti-Oedipus*) detach themselves respectively from Freud's more formalistic version of desire, and the idea of capitalist-desiring machines, only to make desire something even more imposing and universal (the rock and force of life). Foucault, however, insists that the concept of desire is something that is only intelligible within, and produced by, discursive practices and formations—in other words, power precedes both desire and the subject.

Moreover, there is a great deal at stake, for various formations of power, in being able to define, explain and deploy the concept of desire as a form of truth or an aspect of knowledge. As a privileged form of truth, desire authorises socio-cultural narratives and explanations, provides the basis for the categorisation of subjects and their bodies, and is identified as that which must be embraced, affirmed, negated or negotiated if the subject is to achieve self-knowledge, salvation, mental health, bodily pleasure or control, as well as a variety of other objectives. The body of the subject is not so much shaped or brought into being by desire; rather, it is a palimpsest that records and re-records the imposed truths of power. As Butler (1987) writes:

> Foucault's critique of the discourse on desire, on the figure of the 'subjects of desire', does well to remind us that desire is a name that not only accounts for an experience, but determines that experience as well, that the subject of desire may well be a fiction useful to a variety of regulatory strategies . . . If the history of desire must be told in terms of the history of bodies, then it becomes necessary to understand how that history encodes itself in these most immediate phenomena (1987: 238).

This theme of desire as the truth and explanation of the subject has a number of antecedents that predate the great scientific, medical and psychiatric interventions of the nineteenth and twentieth centuries, the most influential of which is Christianity. The recognition of this modern pre-eminence of desire, coupled with the realisation that this situation is inherited from and predicated upon a number of influential discursive regimes and traditions, orients and animates the crucial change of emphasis that takes place from the first to the second and third volumes of *The History of Sexuality*. As Foucault writes:

> it seemed to me that one could not very well analyze the formation and development of the experience of sexuality from the eighteenth century onward, without doing a historical and critical study dealing with desire and the desiring subject. In other words, without undertaking a 'genealogy'. This does not mean that I proposed to write a history of the successive conceptions of desire, of concupiscence, or of libido, but rather to analyze the practices by which individuals were led to focus their attention on themselves, to decipher, recognize, and acknowledge themselves as subjects of desire, bringing into play between themselves and themselves a certain relationship that allows them to discover, in desire, the truth of their being, be it natural or fallen. In short, with this genealogy the idea was to investigate how individuals were led to practice, on themselves and on others, a hermeneutics of desire . . . Thus, in order to understand how the modern individual could experience himself as a subject of a 'sexuality', it was essential first to determine how, for centuries, Western man had been brought to recognize himself as a subject of desire (1985: 5–6).

This genealogical inquiry is characterised by a number of additional but cognate questions about the modern subject—or again, about the way modernity had come to understand and approach that subject. This means considering how contemporary, naturalised ideas and practices gradually emerged from various fields of activity, displacing or effacing other possibilities. The issue that is of particular significance for Foucault is the way in which the Cartesian imperative to 'know thyself' came to be privileged at the expense of the notion of 'the care of the self', even though the latter 'seems to have framed the principle of "know thyself" from the start and to have supported an extremely rich and dense set of notions, practices, ways of being, forms of existence, and so on' (2005: 12). Foucault puts forward a number of explanations to account for this development, such as the Christian notion that salvation can be attained only through self-renunciation, but even here we are faced with the further theoretical questions of how, why, when and in what forms (that is, under what specific set of socio-cultural circumstances and in which manifestations) the imperatives, techniques and dispositions associated with the notion of the care of the self were transformed or superseded by an entirely different, even antithetical, regime. As Foucault makes clear (1997), even the contemporary Californian 'cult of the self' is oriented towards self-discovery, facilitated by scientific knowledge and forms of inquiry (psychoanalysis, psychiatry).

The use of pleasure

All three volumes of *The History of Sexuality* can be characterised as working to bring to light socio-cultural events that enable us to recognise power 'doing its work'—specifically, the establishment, over a considerable period of history, of a particular kind of relationship between the subject and the notion of governmentality that culminates, from the eighteenth century onwards, in the modern subject of desire. The second and third volumes of *The History of Sexuality*, then, do not constitute a major theoretical or methodological break with the first volume—or for that matter with Foucault's work on madness, discipline, discourse, epistemology and power–knowledge. Instead, they constitute a different point of focus, and are simply another way of:

> doing the history of subjectivity; no longer, however, through
> the division between the mad and the nonmad . . . nor through
> the constitution of fields of scientific objectivity . . . but, rather,

through the putting in place, and the transformation in our culture, of 'relations with oneself' (1997: 88).

Foucault begins this inquiry in Classical Greece, with an analysis of what he terms the 'games of truth' that might prove relevant to the analysis of the history of desire and 'the slow formation, in antiquity, of a hermeneutics of the self' (1985: 6). The notion of games of truth, in this context, is not a philosophical inquiry leading to the determination of the true, nor is it a form of knowledge that is attested to and authorised by a field of knowledge. Rather, it refers to the interplay of forms of thought functioning as the means whereby subjects are able to consider, conceive, address and provide an account of themselves— as citizens, workers, men or women, children and/or parents—both to themselves and to the wider community. These forms of thought are only true to the extent that they constitute what is available to, and frame the reality of, the subject, and accordingly delimit the possibilities of subjectivity. However, viewed from another cultural or historical perspective, they often seem both strange and remarkably contingent, much as cultural styles (older styles of acting or singing, and forms of bodily hexis) appear awkward and unnatural to those removed from the contexts that once naturalised them.

One of the main functions—and certainly one of the effects—of Foucault's analysis of sexual behaviour and notions of morality in the Classical Greek world is to produce a sense of estrangement. At the beginning of Part 1 of *The Use of Pleasure*, he points out that, 'One would have a difficult time finding among the Greeks . . . anything resembling the notion of "sexuality"' (1985: 35). The modern concept of sexuality refers to materialities, activities, techniques, forms of knowledge, identities, feelings, pleasures and attitudes that are explicable as a unity in their diversity, or are considered to be 'derived from the same origin' (1985: 35). So sexuality, in this sense, does not separate out or differentiate a set of activities analogous to the Greek concept of *aphrodisia*, the things of Aphrodite (1985: 38), which Foucault translates—with clear difficulty and reservation—as pleasures of love or carnality (1985: 35). He approaches *aphrodisia*, initially, in terms of what it is not: neither a list or set of acts, techniques, norms, categories, interdictions or values, nor the surface play of power, repression or the truth of the self; it is 'neither classification or decipherment' (1985: 38).

This difference between *aphrodisia* and contemporary, Christian and scientific-oriented sexuality is demonstrated via two interrelated observations. First, and contrary to the proliferation of knowledge-based discourses, categories and treatments that Foucault documents in his analysis of nineteenth-century sexuality in the first volume of *The History of Sexuality*, there is a marked absence of an incitement to speak about these things. Foucault acknowledges that this can be attributed to modesty: he observes, with some irony, that Greek writers 'would not have thought it decent to dispense the sort of presumptive and pragmatic advice on sexual relations with one's lawful wife that the Christian authors lavishly distributed on the subject of conjugal pleasures' (1985: 39). At the same time, because carnal activity was not considered to be, as Foucault writes (1985: 40), a 'profound' site, revelatory of the truth of the self, there was less reason to analyse it and make it speak. As a corollary, this so-called privileging of carnality within Christianity gives rise to a suspicion not only of associated feelings such as desire, but also all forms of pleasure and enjoyment. Foucault points to the example from Saint Augustine's *Confessions*, where recollection of the friendships and affections of his youth are reconsidered in the light that 'underneath its seeming innocence, all that did not pertain to the flesh, to that "glue" which attaches us to the flesh' (1985: 40).

Foucault suggests that *aphrodisia* is characterised by a dynamic relationship between desires, acts and pleasures, a relationship that suffers dissociation in the Christian period, when pleasure is simply left without a place in the largely procreation-based arrangement of sexuality. For the Greeks, desire requires satisfaction (acts), which give rise to pleasure; and the pleasure derived from such acts in turn fuels desire, and so on. The focus of ethical inquiry, for Plato, Aristotle and other contemporary Greek philosophers, is not so much the types of acts (although there is a regime regarding the appropriateness of certain acts and techniques in the wider contexts of the age, gender and social status of the participants), or the extent to which such acts could be considered concomitant with nature (although, as Foucault admits, Plato 'draws a sharp opposition' (1985: 44) between hetero- and homosexual relationships). Rather, what is deemed unnatural is self-indulgence, understood as a departure from moderation and balance—in other words, a quantitative excess of energy of force directed to or expended on a particular activity or object of desire. Given that *aphrodisia* is located within the natural order, it therefore cannot of itself be considered immoral except in that it constitutes a surfeit, a fault that could be characteristic of other desires or needs, such as those involving food and drink. However, to some extent carnality is differentiated from these by the level of intensity directed at the activity/object. It was this:

> natural acuteness of pleasure, together with the attraction that it exerted on desire, that caused sexual activity to go beyond the limits that were set by nature . . . people were led to go beyond the satisfaction of needs and to continue looking for pleasure even after the body had been restored. Nature had invested human beings with this necessary and redoubtable force, which was always on the point of overshooting the objective that was set for it (1985: 49–50).

The problem of carnal excess was not simply reduced to a question of economics—although spending more than was required or advisable in one area of activity clearly had detrimental consequences elsewhere. Of greater concern was the notion that it presaged or disposed a general irresponsibility and carelessness with regard both to the care of the self, and more widely to one's duties as citizen, parent, teacher, soldier or ruler. Foucault makes the point that *aphrodisia* was to some extent regarded as an inferior set of pleasures because it was more closely associated with animalistic behaviour, and therefore had within it the potential to overthrow the direction provided by reason and the soul. The relationship between desire, sexual activity and pleasure was thus a serious subject requiring an ethos or morality—one not motivated, as with Christianity, by the notion of sin or a fall, but rather by the need for the kind of self-control and self-management that enabled subjects to exercise reasoned rule over themselves and their families, and to contribute to the well-being of the community. As Foucault explains it, the ethical questions that applied to the field of *aphrodisia* were of the order of a regimen, style and pragmatics rolled into one:

> How does a man enjoy his pleasure 'as he ought'? To what principles does he refer in order to moderate, limit, regulate that activity? What sort of validity might these principles have that would enable a man to justify his having to obey them? Or, in other words, what is the mode of subjection that is implied in this moral problematization of sexual conduct (1985: 53)?

Three main factors that informed this regimen-as-ethics: need, timeliness and status. With regard to the issue of need, Foucault refers to Diogenes' scandalous but, in his own terms and those of his followers (Cynics), perfectly logical habit of masturbating in public, his reasoning being that as sexual activity was nothing more than an act that addressed and satisfied a pressing natural need, it could be performed openly—much like eating or drinking. Moreover, the notion of treating sexual desire as a need and avoiding immoderate or unnatural levels or forms of activity constituted an art, since it was presumed that the intensity of enjoyment was related to self-limitation. By way of analogy, Foucault refers to Xenophon's account of Socrates, who 'found appetite the best sauce; and any kind of drink he found pleasant,

147

because he drank only when he was thirsty' (1985: 57). This linkage of *aphrodisia* and art is equally applicable to the notion of timeliness: different categories of time (seasons, human age, the daily cycles of the body) determined, favoured or worked against the productivity, benefit and pleasure derived from sexual activity (in terms of the relation between age and procreation, climate and intercourse, or work and recreation). So, according to Socrates, the fact that the offspring of parent–child incest must come to a bad end is partly explained by the inappropriate difference in age—that is, because 'parents failed to respect the principle of the "right time", mixing their seed unseasonably, since one of them was necessarily much older than the other' (1985: 59). Finally, the art of pleasure also applied to sexual conduct between different social categories of subjects, although not in a manner that would be recognisable with post-Christian moral conventions or rules (involving, most obviously, the categories of the married and unmarried). In Classical Greek (and not just Athenian) culture, this took a more fluid and pragmatic turn—for instance, taking the form of a presumed correspondence between those who exercised command over, or held positions of considerable responsibility with regard to, the community, and the requirement of an exemplary, restrained and moderate sexual disposition.

What these various regimens, pragmatics, styles and arts testify to, for Foucault, is that:

> We are a long way from a form of austerity that would tend to govern all individuals in the same way . . . under a universal law . . . On the contrary, here everything was a matter of adjustment, circumstance, and personal position. The few common laws—of the city, religion, nature—remained present, but it was as if they traced a very wide circle in the distance, inside of which practical thought had to define what could rightfully be done. And for this there was no need of anything resembling a text that would have the force of law, but rather a

techne . . . a *savoir-faire* that by taking general principles into account would guide action in its time, according to its context, and in view of its ends (1985: 62).

The care of the self

Foucault exemplifies this last point—concerning what we might call the utility associated with and derived from this regimen—by way of a close analysis (2005) of Plato's text *Alcibiades*. Foucault points out (2005: 66) that the Socratic exchanges in Plato's text cannot stand in for nor adequately address the complexities of the history and discourses of the concept of the care of the self in Classical Greece. Nevertheless, *Alcibiades* constitutes a 'landmark' and a 'reference point in classical philosophy' (2005: 66), and therefore provides a useful introductory point for a consideration of the subject. Plato relates how Socrates approaches the rich, powerful, beautiful and much-admired Alcibiades, and asks him whether he'd prefer to die young, or live on without attaining glory. Alcibiades answers that he would rather die than live a life in which he neither achieves nor contributes anything of note or significance. Socrates understands that Alcibiades is expressing more than a desire to attract honour and fame—he wants to turn his privileged position (his nobility, family connections and wealth) into some form of political activity, which would see him leading and governing his fellow citizens. This is where 'the question of the care of the self arises' (2005: 33). If Alcibiades is to govern the city, he must overcome formidable obstacles; he has both internal competition and powerful enemies (Sparta, Persia) abroad. Socrates asks Alcibiades 'to reflect on himself a little, to review his life and compare himself with his rivals. A counsel of prudence: Think a bit about who you are in comparison with those you want to confront and you will discover your inferiority' (2005: 35).

Alcibiades is not only inferior in wealth and power compared with his rivals; he is also less well educated: Socrates demonstrates to him that he is deficient in what Foucault refers to as techne and *savoir-faire* (2005: 35), and this disqualifies him from governing. This leads to the question of what precisely is required if one is to govern well, and how we can recognise it. After the usual backwards and forwards movements of Socratic dialogue:

> We end up with the definition advanced by Alcibiades: The city is well governed when harmony reigns among its citizens. Alcibiades is asked: What is this harmony; in what does it consist? Alcibiades cannot answer . . . and he despairs . . . To this Socrates responds: Don't worry; if you were to discover your shameful ignorance . . . when you are fifty, it really would be difficult to remedy, because it would be very difficult to take care of yourself (2005: 35).

The care of oneself is not something derived from or innate to privilege; rather—and specifically in the case of Alcibiades—it involves an overcoming of privilege, a moving beyond the limitations of thought, attitude and disposition that privilege has accorded. Taking care of oneself, in this sense, means investigating the extent to which the habitus of wealth and power leads to the subject taking the right to govern for granted. It also involves learning how to discriminate regarding what constitutes self-care in various social contexts and activities, including the field of *aphrodisia*. Finally, the disposition to take care of the self must be integrated into the sensibility of the subject as a reflex, which involves calling into question or testing the extent to which activities (political, sexual, familial) lead us to, prepare us for and facilitate our communal responsibilities.

The care of the self, as it is presented in Foucault's reading of the first part of *Alcibiades*, is largely characterised by five inter-related activities-as-process—overcoming, testing, discriminating, transforming and learning. What remains to be addressed in the second half of Plato's text is how this process is to come about—in other words, what it is that allows the subject to do these things, and thereby move from a state of ignorance to one of wisdom. The answer, which when it is given is 'one of the decisive moments of the text, one of the constitutive moments . . . of Platonism, and . . . one of those fundamental episodes in the history of the technologies of the self . . . consists in knowing oneself' (2005: 67). Foucault suggests that whereas after Descartes (and more generally, for modernity) the imperative to know thyself came to be privileged over and to marginalise the notion of the care of the self, in Classical Greece they still form 'a dynamic entanglement'—and remain so through Roman and Hellenistic times, although with certain variations and different points of emphasis (2005: 68).

How is the subject to come to an understanding of (that is, see and recognise) its true being—the term used by Foucault in the text is 'soul'? He maintains that the only way is through recourse to the divine (the gods, thought and knowledge), which is the source of the soul; therefore, 'One must know the divine in order to know oneself . . . the soul will be endowed with wisdom . . . as soon as it is in contact with the divine' (2005: 71). Being initiated into wisdom as a way of seeing, the subject can then turn back from the divine to the world and govern because, being transformed (made wise), they can now discriminate and evaluate (identify what is good and bad, distinguish and judge what is true from what is false). There is one further move, however, one gloss on the notion of the divine that Foucault identifies in Alcibiades' final promise to Socrates before he sets off to govern the Athenians. He promises to apply himself not to the care of himself, but to justice. As Foucault writes, 'that was the point of the dialogue . . . to convince Alcibiades that . . . taking care of oneself and being concerned with justice amount to the same thing' (2005: 72).

Self-testing, training and *askesis*

Alcibiades learns that the disposition to take care of the self must be adopted as a reflex, which involves and requires constant self-interrogation, testing and training—in other words, it is not enough simply to want to do right, or to know which principles are the right ones. The name the Greeks gave to this notion of a regime of self-testing and training was *askesis*. The idea was that, just as a successful athlete must constantly train and exercise in order to overcome their limitations, so Alcibiades could only govern the city if he was able to overcome the challenges involved in governing—which meant being in the right shape, figuratively speaking. So the fact that Alcibiades eventually failed to perform his duties properly cannot be attributed to Socrates' teaching; rather, 'after all his successes with men, women, and a whole populace made him a champion . . . he thought he could neglect his training' (2005: 72).

In his introduction to *The Use of Pleasure*, Foucault asserts that it would be 'a mistake to infer that the sexual morality of Christianity and that of paganism formed a continuity' (1985: 20–1). However, he goes on to suggest that 'very early in the moral thought of antiquity, a thematic complex . . . of sexual austerity . . . formed around and apropos of the life of the body . . . and the existence of wisdom' (1985: 21); and 'crossing through institutions, sets of precepts . . . diverse theoretical references, and in spite of many alterations, this thematics maintained a certain constancy' (1985: 21–2). This is clear even in the relatively homogeneous context of Classical Greece, where the account of *askesis* was developed and varied at a level of function and intensity that depended on the philosophical tradition in question (Platonic, Pythagorean, Stoic, Cynic). However, what the various traditions shared was a tendency not to codify these exercises of self-control. This was the case, Foucault explains, for two main reasons: first, the exercises were more or less indistinguishable from the ends to be achieved (the ability to endure hunger comes via a regime of rationing, bravery through exposure to simulated danger); and second, because those ends were themselves considered to be generic, and therefore the benefits were transferable (so learning to govern oneself or one's family equipped a subject to govern the community).

Foucault argues that the principles and techniques of the care of the self were relatively constant and homogeneous in Classical Greece, although allowances would need to be made for context-specific variations and different forms of emphasis. This situation changes, to some extent, in the Hellenistic and Roman periods. The procedures and techniques of *askesis*, for instance, were 'greatly amplified'; they were subject to increased codification, organisation and categorisation, and became a 'subject matter for teaching and constituted one of the basic instruments used in the direction of souls' (1985: 74). Foucault provides the following, more general, account of these changes, from which Christianity was to 'borrow extensively':

> A mistrust of the pleasures, an emphasis on the consequences of their abuse for the body and the soul, a valorization of marriage and marital obligations, a disaffection with regard to the spiritual meanings imputed to the love of boys: a whole attitude of severity was manifested in the thinking of philosophers and physicians in the course of the first two centuries . . . More precisely, there was a greater apprehension concerning the sexual pleasures, more attention given to the relation that one might have with them. In a word, there was a more intense problematization of the *aphrodisia* (1986a: 39).

Foucault makes the point that, apart from occasional exceptions such as Rome under the rule of Augustus, this tendency towards austerity and severity did not usually result in legislative or juridical intervention; nor was there a uniform move to a more strict or rigorous regimen of behaviour. The most significant difference was one of attitude and disposition. Foucault refers to the argument that whereas for the philosophies of Classical Greece the ultimate end of the care of the self was tied up with one's relation to the community (we recall that Alcibiades is driven, first and foremost, by a sense of duty with regard to the city and its citizens), in the Hellenistic and Roman periods there is a weakening of socio-political relations and frameworks that were afforded by and derived from the fact that in Classical Greece most citizens lived in close proximity to one another, in the city. This brought about a turn to individualism that 'accorded more and more importance to the "private" aspect of existence, to the values of personal conduct, and to the interest that people focused on themselves' (1986a: 41). While acknowledging that 'not everything is false in a schema of this sort' (1986a: 41), Foucault is suspicious of this explanation, for a variety of reasons—including the point that Hellenistic and Roman societies were characterised by strong communal and familial frameworks, at least for the upper classes; and the fact that the Stoics, who outdid other groups in their doctrinal commitment to personal austerity, were also the most community oriented.

Foucault's response is to problematise the notion of individualism itself, pointing out that the term is often applied, as in the case above, in a manner that treats different attitudes, foci and intensities as if they referred to the same realities, or were more or less contiguous. He identifies and separates out three main aspects of Hellenistic and Roman attitudes that are read as signs of individualism, and that are often and unnecessarily 'lumped together' (1986a: 42): first, the notion of the individual being independent with regard to the community, with this relationship being accorded a high level of cultural capital; second, particular value being placed on familial and domestic life and activities; and third, what Foucault refers to as an 'intensity of the relations to self' (1986a: 42), a situation marked by a tendency to focus attention upon and seek out the meanings of the self, in order to 'transform, correct, and purify oneself, and find salvation' (1986a: 42). Foucault points out that there is no necessary articulation between or across these phenomena, making reference to a number of examples—for instance, aristocratic warrior castes that prize individualism but attach no great value to domestic life; and the Christian ascetic movement of the first century that accentuated and intensified one's relation to the self, 'but in a form of a disqualification of the values of private life . . . and an explicit rejection of any individualism' (1986a: 43).

The cultivation of the self

We quoted Foucault to the effect that the imperative to know thyself and the notion of the care of the self formed 'a dynamic entanglement' (1985: 68) in Classical Greece, and that this remained the case through Roman and Hellenistic times. It is with regard to the changes to and variations in this relationship that Foucault explains the 'demands of sexual austerity in imperial times' (1986a: 43) not as a general individualism, but in terms of the 'development of what might be called a "cultivation of the self", wherein the relations of oneself to oneself were intensified and valorized' (1986a: 43). This notion of the cultivation of the self, although only applying to a small and privileged elite, served a similar function—in form if not in scale—to the 'repression hypothesis' of the nineteenth century—that is to say, it was a discursive regime that organised practices; created institutions and bodies of knowledge; gave rise to taxonomies, categories, pedagogies, procedures and techniques of behaviour and exercise; influenced or determined forms of subjectivity; and set the parameters—what Foucault refers to as the 'games of truth'—through and by which the subject understood and experienced reality.

This imperial version of the care of the self can be distinguished from its predecessors in four main ways. First, the strong emphasis that is placed on, and the privileging of, self-care as art—a tendency that is already present, to a marked extent, in Platonic thought—is seen to be realised through recourse to established and authorised formulae, procedures and rules. Second, there is an increase both in the use of medical discourse with regard to the techniques, aims and ends of philosophical exercise (prescribing, amputating, soothing), and as a logical corollary, a pathologising of metaphysical and mental issues and problems: Epictetus tells his disciples that if 'You wish to learn syllogism . . . You must first attend to your ulcers, and stay your flux, and arrive at peace in your mind' (1986a: 55); and the physician Galen considered it 'within his competence not only to cure the great aberrations of the mind . . . but to treat the passions . . . and the errors' (1986a: 56). Third, the regimes of *askesis*—testing, self-examination, sets of exercises—increasingly are oriented towards the production of knowledge that will facilitate a discovery of the truth of the self. Fourth, in the field of *aphrodisia* there is a move from an emphasis being placed on the balance and economies of force that need to inform the uses of pleasure, to a need to protect the self against debilitating exposure, as well as on the susceptibility of the subject. As Foucault writes:

> One is still far from an experience of sexual pleasure where the latter will be associated with evil, where behavior will have to submit to the universal form of the law, and where the deciphering of desire will be a necessary condition for acceding to a purified existence. Yet one can already see how the question of evil begins to work upon the ancient theme of force, how the question of law begins to modify the theme of art and techne, and how the question of truth and the principles of self-knowledge evolve within the ascetic practices (1986a: 68).

The question of salvation

In *The Hermeneutics of the Subject* (2005), a collection of lectures delivered at the Collège de France in 1981–82, Foucault offers a very detailed and somewhat revised account, predicated on a reading of the Platonic, Epicurean and Stoic (or at least the school specific to Epictetus) versions of the care of the self, of the major points of transition from Classical Greece to Hellenistic and Imperial Rome. He returns to and considers the content of *Alcibiades*, and reminds his audience that the Athenian needed to learn to take care of himself in order to govern the city wisely and justly—in other words, 'care of the self is therefore instrumental with regard to care of others' (2005: 175). In order to more fully demonstrate this, Foucault points to the counter example of Plato's *Symposium*, where a drunken Alcibiades confesses that he has undertaken the governance of the Athenians without a concomitant commitment to self-care, with predictable results; as Foucault writes, 'All the dramas and disasters of the real Alcibiades are picked out in this little gap between the promise of the Alcibiades and the drunkenness of the *Symposium*' (2005: 175).

This connection between self-care and the ability to take care of others is characterised as a necessary imbrication of what neo-Platonism refers to as the cathartic and the political (2005: 176). This linkage has three main stages. The first stage is tendentious: I undergo catharsis (understood as the purification and transformation of the self) in order to become a political subject (who understands politics and is capable of governing). The second stage is reciprocal: if I govern well and 'ensure salvation and prosperity for my fellow citizens', then as a member of that community I also benefit from 'the city's salvation' (2005: 176). The third and final stage is one of realisation or recognition: in moving from the first to the second stages, I come to understand that the personal and the communal are inextricably linked, and that the salvation of the subject is always predicated on saving the city. This is 'roughly the link Plato establishes between care of the self and care of others, and . . . in such a way that it is very difficult to separate them' (2005: 176). Foucault suggests that by the Roman period 'this separation has . . . been broadly carried out' (2005: 176): the notion of the care of the self is transformed into an end in itself, characterised by an emphasis on purely cathartic issues, the cultivation of the self, self-forming as art, and the transformation of philosophy into spirituality (2005: 179). He writes that:

> You can see that from this also arises the fact that when Christian spirituality develops in its strictest ascetic and monastic form, from the third and fourth centuries, it can present itself quite naturally as the fulfilment of an ancient, pagan philosophy . . . The ascetic life . . . will be the true philosophy . . . in the direct line of a *tekhne* that had become an art of oneself (2005: 178).

Up to this point (in the lectures from *The Hermeneutics of the Subject*), Foucault has concentrated on explaining and showing how this change in the Hellenistic and Roman periods has appeared in the discourses of various schools of philosophy (Epicurean, Stoic, Pythagorean). However, he widens the scope of both his inquiry (paying attention to historical, social and cultural documents) and his claims by suggesting that from the Hellenistic period onwards we are dealing with the development of a culture of the self (2005: 179). He points to the presence of four conditions that would enable us to use the term 'culture' in this context. First, it is made up of a relatively loose regime of values that give rise to, perpetuate and consecrate hierarchies. Second, these values are universalised, but remain the domain of the privileged. Third, these values are to be attained through what Pierre Bourdieu would call the condition and sensibility of illusion (2000), whereby the subject completely and unthinkingly identifies with, believes in and inhabits them. Fourth, there is a familiarity and literacy with regard to the relevant fields of knowledge, understood as a system and both developed through bodily activities (techniques, exercises, regimes) and manifested in the bodily hexis (as a particular way of moving, and deploying and carrying the body). Foucault privileges this Hellenistic culture of the self with considerable significance, claiming that:

it is hardly possible to undertake the history of subjectivity, of the relations between the subject and truth, without setting it in the framework of this culture of the self that afterwards, in Christianity . . . and then in the Renaissance and the seventeenth century, undergoes a series of changes and transformations (2005: 180).

What are the elements of this culture of the self that Foucault posits as leading, through Christianity, humanism and the rise of the human sciences, and the advent of the reason of state, to the modern conception of the subject? Foucault places emphasis on two particular aspects: the meanings and functions that come to be associated with the idea of salvation; and the relation between the subject and truth. Foucault introduces the Hellenistic and Roman versions of what is understood by salvation by first separating them from what they are not. The Platonic idea of salvation is a somewhat distant relative, largely because it functions almost entirely as a philosophical rather than what Foucault refers to as a spiritual concept—and even then it lacks 'specific and strict meaning' (2005: 180).

In Christianity, the opposite is true: salvation is informed strongly by a binary logic, always referring to some kind of movement from a fallen, abject, ignorant or corrupted state (identified with sin, death, mortality, despair, evil), to something infinitely finer and better (grace, everlasting life, certainty, goodness). It is understood as the moment or occasion of a passage from a world and state of temporality and flesh to something that is eternal and purely spiritual. In the Hellenistic and Imperial texts studied by Foucault, however, salvation refers to a process whereby the subject attains a degree of control and peace, ensuring both an 'absence of inner turmoil' (with regard to needs, pleasures, desires, etc.) and a defence against 'misfortunes, disorders, and . . . external accidents' (2005: 184). The subject becomes to some extent self-sufficient: salvation is neither tied to the other nor predicated on self-renunciation. The question of the subject's relation to the salvation of the other doesn't exactly disappear, but rather undergoes 'a reversal' (2005: 192): the care of the self is now carried out specifically for and through the self, and 'The benefit for others, the salvation of others . . . comes as a supplementary . . . reward for the operation and activity of the salvation you exercise with perseverance on yourself' (2005: 192).

This turning of one's gaze and attention from the other to the self in the Hellenistic and Imperial periods is, for Foucault, 'right at the heart of the problem' of the 'relationship between truth-telling and governing' (2005: 229). Foucault refers to a theme in Classical Greek thought whereby knowledge of the world is privileged over, and considered a prerequisite for attaining, knowledge of men; and he argues that this theme is taken up and developed by the Cynics, Epicureans, Stoics and Pythagoreans (2005: 230). For the Cynics (Foucault refers to the ideas of the philosopher Demetrius as they are reported by Seneca, and takes them as being representative of the School in the Imperial period), knowledge is divided between the useless, superfluous or distracting (understood loosely as knowledge of the things of nature, of material measurements and of causal relations), and what we might call meta-knowledge, which involves an understanding of the subject's relation to and place within the universe. This meta-knowledge has three main aspects—it is prescriptive, functional and ethical: the prescriptions (despise the embellishments of life, there is nothing to fear in death) produce an effect on the subject (bringing calm, peace, certainty) and, as a consequence, they transform the subject's practices (producing an ethics, a different way of relating to others).

Foucault argues that much the same notion and logic can be found in Epicurean, Stoic and Pythagorean thought: rather than valuing and valorising self-knowledge as an end in itself, and the basis of our salvation, we are disposed to value knowledge of certain principles that reorient us and our relation to the world, and produce us as ethical subjects. In these terms:

Knowledge of the self . . . is not then on the way to becoming the decipherment of the mysteries of conscience and the exegesis of the self which developed later in Christianity. Useful knowledge, knowledge in which human life is at stake, is a relational mode of knowledge that asserts and prescribes at the same time and is capable of producing a change in the subject's mode of being (2005: 237–8).

Self-knowledge

Foucault argues that the exercises, self-examinations and self-preparations of Cynic and related schools of philosophy of this period effect a 'double decoupling' of the relationship between *askesis* and self-knowledge that previously characterised Platonic and neo-Platonic thought (2005: 420). The first part of this process removes self-knowledge from 'the central axis of the *askesis*' (2005: 420): its place is now occupied by the precepts that allow the subject to deal with and overcome (or at least remain unmoved with regard to) the vicissitudes of everyday life, in much the same way that a well-prepared athlete is able to meet all the challenges of a contest (2005: 322). The second change involves a shift away from the notion, central to Plato and neo-Platonism, and still largely retained by the Stoics, that self-knowledge is derived from recognition of the divine within oneself. Foucault suggests this double 'decoupling'—of *askesis* and self-knowledge, and self-knowledge and the divine—'was at the source of the historical success of these exercises, of their historical success, paradoxically, in Christianity itself' (2005: 420).

Foucault insists that this break does not produce anything that could be mistaken for the Christian version of *askesis*, but it does anticipate and facilitate it. He demonstrates this by way of reference to the trope of the athlete as it functions in the two orders of discourse. In Stoic thought, the athlete is to be differentiated from other practitioners of physical exercise, such as the dancer. Whereas the dancer works towards embodying a certain ideal that requires surpassing or leaving the self behind, the activities, thoughts and bodily hexis of the wrestler in competition are always attuned to the relation between the intersection of the self and the moment. The Christian athlete, on the other hand, is in some ways like the dancer:

> The Christian athlete is on the indefinite path of progress towards holiness in which he must surpass himself even to the point of renouncing himself. Also, the Christian athlete is especially someone who has an enemy . . . who keeps him on guard. With regard to whom and to what? But with regard to himself! To himself, inasmuch as the most malign and dangerous powers he has to confront (sin, fallen nature, seduction by the devil, etcetera) are within himself. The Stoic athlete . . . has to be ready for a struggle in which his adversary is . . . coming to him from the external world . . . The ancient athlete is an athlete of the event. The Christian is an athlete of himself (2005: 322).

The two main points of connection between these otherwise quite different regimes are that, first, Christianity inherits what Foucault terms 'the old Stoic suspicion towards oneself' (2005: 422); and second, Christianity takes on and develops the important role accorded to the master and guide in Stoic thought and activity. The ascetic exercises of the Stoic athlete were to proliferate under Christianity: manuals of exercises, devotions and procedures, and regimes of abstinence and sacrifice, all woven into the fabric of the subject's daily life, from morning to night and from birth to death; prescribed and specified in terms of quantity, temporality and intensity; and inscribed with a direction, a function, a narrative of utility. The Christian athlete (who in time becomes a soldier) will be even better prepared than the Stoic, being equipped with the extra advantage of a much more imposing and authoritative corpus of texts, rules and techniques; the Christian adheres to, lives out and manifests the rules (the word of God) that lead to salvation. Moreover, this path to salvation is not only signposted everywhere and every day; a variety of institutionally authorised guides also exist to advise, support, encourage and, where necessary, rebuke. This is perhaps where Christianity departs most radically from the ethos and practices of the care of the self that characterise Classical Greece. As Foucault writes:

> From the moment that the culture of the self was taken up by Christianity, it was . . . put to work for the exercise of . . . pastoral power . . . insofar as individual salvation is channelled—to a certain extent, at least—through a pastoral institution that has the care of the soul as its object, the classical care of the self disappeared, that is, was integrated and lost a large part of its autonomy (1997: 278).

Technologies of the self

In the three volumes of *The History of Sexuality*, and in earlier works such as *The Birth of the Clinic* and *Discipline and Punish*, Foucault provides a genealogical account of these epistemic shifts in the subject's relation to the self, and to power and broader society, through a consideration of what he terms the four major types of technology through which we operate. They are:

> (1) technologies of production, which permit us to produce, transform, or manipulate things; (2) technologies of sign systems, which permit us to use signs, meanings, symbols, or signification; (3) technologies of power, which determine the conduct of individuals and submit them to certain ends or domination, an objectivizing of the subject; (4) technologies of

the self, which permit individuals to effect by their own means or with the help of others a certain number of operations on their own bodies and souls, thoughts, conduct, and way of being, so as to transform themselves in order to attain a certain state of happiness, purity, wisdom, perfection, or immortality (1980: 18).

The first and second technologies allow societies to function in practical terms, through production and communication. The technologies of power—those mechanisms that both produce and regulate human subjects—are the focus of Foucault's earlier work. In *The Birth of the Clinic* and *Discipline and Punish*, he examines how the technologies of power confine and constrain individuals. In *The History of Sexuality*, he changes tack, and examines how subjects use the technologies of the self to confine and constrain themselves. Technologies of the self are internalised mechanisms of power, in contrast to technologies of power, which are brought to bear on us from outside. They are the many ways in which we as individuals engage with the laws and norms of our culture, respond to the discourses and the forces of power that have shaped our identity and sense of self, and thereby manage ourselves.

We can make sense of this by discussing a contemporary 'social problem'—obesity. Increasingly, obesity is seen as the major health issue in industrialised societies at least—though it is becoming recognised as such in developing nations as well. The World Health Organization (WHO) has produced figures showing that, worldwide, there are over a billion overweight adults and 22 million children under five who are overweight. The WHO, along with the medical field, has identified a direct link between obesity and chronic diseases (WHO 2003), and there have also been links observed between obesity and both psychological and social problems. Because of the perception that there is an 'obesity epidemic', food and diet are becoming important sites for determining what constitutes acceptable forms of subjectivity. This is not the first time in history that food has taken such a role; Foucault notes that food and diet were important during the Roman epoch—even more important than sex (1986a: 141)—because right living, or in this case, right eating, was central to the notion of taking care of the self. In the contemporary world, this operates via the suggestion that people are overweight or obese as a direct result of a lack of self-control, a lack of discipline; and they are a risk to society because of their status as self-induced chronic invalids who also fail to satisfy the norms of physical appearance.

While it seems self-evident that there are health problems associated with carrying too much weight, it is probably reasonable to suggest that Foucault would read the problem of obesity not simply as one of health, but as one in which those who are overweight are seen as having failed to comply with the rules for 'right' behaviour and being. We can extrapolate from Foucault's comments on another public health issue to consider how his work might address the problem of obesity. He refers to the example of parasitosis in Brazil, and acknowledges that it is certainly a public health problem, but points out that any treatment is likely to be accompanied by the imposition of 'a type of medical power, and a type of relationship to the body, and a type of authoritarianism—a system of obedience' (1988b: 195). In other words, in our age we do not treat health issues simply as such, but rather as issues of managing the whole self through compliance with regard to medical dictates. Clinical regimes are necessarily tied to, and facilitated by, the workings of power, while remaining couched in terms of the logics, imperatives and discourses of science. This is the case with overweight and obese people, and their diagnosis and treatment. The process will have a number of related stages: (1) categorise and name the data (concerning a trend in the number of people exceeding a 'normal' body weight) as an epidemic; (2) shame the overweight and obese through frequent reportage of the 'problem', illustrated by film of their bellies and buttocks; (3) point out the health issues to themselves, the burden on their families and on the public health system; and (4) institute rules and regulations to manage the problem. Because obesity is constantly named as a problem, a crisis or an epidemic, those identified as 'problem subjects' are forced to reflect on their own identity and their own practices, and ideally will bring themselves into line with social norms. This is an example of the interiorising of the technologies of power—a transfer of power's force from direct action to the technologies of the self. Self-discipline and self-surveillance are the keys here. Under this economy of power, designed to produce docile bodies and 'good subjects':

> There is no need for arms, physical violence, material constraints. Just a gaze. An inspecting gaze, a gaze which each individual under its weight will end by interiorising it to the point that he is his own overseer, each individual thus exercising this surveillance over, and against himself (1980: 155).

This is directly and indirectly applied to the public, but very directly when it comes to children and their diets and bodily regimes. Childhood obesity is presented as a particular social problem, and schools are charged with tackling the issue. One of the tools used is the surveillance of children's eating habits—not the control of what they eat, as would be possible if schools provided lunches, but more subtly by teachers observing and responding to the lunches children bring from home. Deana Leahy (2010) points out that there has been over a century of attention paid by schools to children's diets, and that schools increasingly are required to intervene in children's food choices. Not only are children educated with regard to the food pyramid, various nutrients and components of foodstuffs, but in some states policies control what children may eat or drink during school hours, and their lunchboxes are policed. Even if the intervention is less direct, it can still be very potent. Leahy notes that in some schools, teachers will patrol the eating areas and point out the 'gold star' lunches (wholegrain bread, salads and fruit), or criticise lunchboxes containing 'unhealthy' food—soft drinks instead of water, for instance, or crisps or cakes instead of fruit. This public observation, and the associated public approbation or opprobrium signalled through the teacher's response, is a very powerful way of reinforcing the discourses of health and diet, and of reminding subjects (in this case, schoolchildren and their parents) that they are not autonomous, but are literally subject to external power.

Subjectivity, normalisation and everyday practice

For Foucault, the subject only emerges by way of the workings of the discourses, categories and procedures of power, and so 'juridical systems of power produce the subjects they subsequently come to represent' (Butler 1990: 2). This means that all forms of identity are based on and linked to social and legal procedures, processes, techniques, norms and structures. In order to have, gain, claim or be assigned an identity, an individual must be recognisable and explicable within a grid of intelligibility that both makes the subject appear, and authorises that subject's status as an identity-in-waiting. The production of subjectivity is effected when the subject's body becomes explicable within socio-cultural and/or scientific discursive categories: the body is designated as being commensurate with, or failing to satisfy, the terms of those categories, and the person is thus inscribed in terms of certain meanings, values, dispositions, orientations and narratives.

How does the body figure within the context of the constitutive powers and work performed by normative discourses? We can understand this by considering something seemingly as obvious, unmediated and commonsensical as the parts of the body—the stomach, arms, feet, neck or genitals, for instance. All these parts are only distinctive in terms of their relation to, and differentiation from, other parts of the overall structure. In everyday popular (rather than physiological) understanding, it can be said that the stomach begins somewhere below the chest and ends above the groin and the genitals, and reaches its limits on either side at the hips (below) and the ribs (above), while there is that disconcertingly anonymous area in between that attracts the designation of 'the side'. This is obviously very vague when compared with the explanation offered by the physiological sciences, but while the categories, points of differentiation and specific characteristics that define the parts of the body in scientific discourse are more definite than are those offered by popular discourse, they too are imprecise. The charts that neatly plot and represent the parameters and locations of organs, muscles, ligaments, blood vessels and bones disguise the reality that spaces are blurred or shared, categories overlap, and imbrication rather than separation is the reality.

When considering how the parts of the body are seen, we have to remember that the various systems of categorisation, explication and representation—the everyday, the scientific, the quasi-scientific, the religious, the culinary—are at best connected to and translatable into one another by way of a vague family resemblance, rather than rigorous scientific equation or correspondence. Moreover, this lack of correspondence across systems of categorisation is even more pronounced when we take into account historical and technological differences. The scientific body clearly feeds into and influences the popular version of the body, but in periods prior to the emergence of science (or, for that matter, writing), the body, at the level of the commonsensical and everyday, was categorised, organised and recognised in ways that would have been unthinkable to the contemporary world.

For Foucault, systems of categorisation don't just arrange content: they both naturalise a certain mediated version of the world, and simultaneously render anything else more or less unthinkable. A thing can be identified only when it can be assigned meaning—that is to say, when it can be recognised and classified as being normal, or otherwise. Every discursive regime—and every order of truth—is predicated on this relationship between evaluation and identification. Subjects are only identifiable as humans because at a certain time, in a certain place, for certain institutions they are characterised by markers and performances that have been assimilated into, and institutionalised as, authorised cultural categories (involving, say, gender, age, class, race, ethnicity and bodily hexis). In fact, we follow Judith Butler (who is herself following Foucault) on this point and say that, paradoxically, materiality only comes into being through the facility of cultural discourses and categories of perception that are themselves dependent on, and recognisable via, the process of iteration (Butler 1993). Discursive regimes always call up that which they produce as evidence of their own authority and legitimacy. As Slavoj Žižek (1991) shows, the law always makes use of the effects of the law, and then claims to treat and evaluate, disinterestedly, what it finds before it.

The reproduction and continuation of normalised ways of seeing and behaving in a sense constitute a circular process: social fields, institutions, techniques and mechanisms produce subjects who are inclined to see and understand the world, and everyone in it, in terms of recognisable and authorised categories, and the templates that go with them. Butler (1990, 1993, 2005) suggests that this process is facilitated via authorised, iterative performances of normalisation. Her argument is that there are sites in a culture (most particularly the media but also, more conventionally, sites and institutions such as schools, the family and work) where we can monitor whether our subjectivity is 'on track' in terms of our body shape, clothes, mannerisms, or ways of seeing and evaluating other people. These images, ideas and performances constitute a vast store of up-to-date templates for, or models of, a normal, healthy, attractive and desirable subject. Such evaluation and categorisation of each and every subject, including the self, represent 'neither a single act nor a causal process initiated by the subject . . . Construction not only takes place in time, but is itself a temporal process which operates through the reiteration of norms' (1993: 10).

The media-as-spectacle and normalisation

Cultural texts, such as advertisements, television shows, films and video games, are populated by types who demonstrate, consistently and insistently, what is attractive and desirable, healthy and normal. But they do more than offer up role-model bodies—they help subjects understand, negotiate and see the world. This form of normative training takes place within pop cultural texts such as magazines and television but also—and usually in considerably less overt manifestations—in more 'serious' texts such as newspaper articles, and scientific or government reports. The media, for instance, provide a huge standing reserve of desires and performances, a kind of mass market of subjectivities from which viewers can theoretically 'pick and choose'. The reality, of course, is somewhat more complex; as Butler points out, the performances of subjectivity that are made available in the media, and the provision of the role models and exemplars that do a great deal of the work of naturalising those performances, are always derived from and commensurate with regimes of normalisation.

This increasingly important role of the commercial media in the production of normalised subjectivities directs us back to the issue that Foucault raises towards the end of *The Birth of Biopolitics*: to what extent is the dominance of neo-liberal and capitalist imperatives, values, discourses and logics in the west likely to inflect or even transform practices and regimes of disciplinarity, normalisation and biopower (2008)? This question has been taken up by Jonathan Crary (1998, 2000), who argues for the need to reconcile Foucault's theories with Guy Debord's account of the politics of the media spectacle.

Debord's ideas and arguments have been highly influential, if only because they have helped draw attention to the ways in which media technology and media as popular culture have increasingly been involved in social and public sphere roles and functions. Crary addresses the media in his discussion, in *Suspensions of Perception*, of the relation between Foucault's work and Guy Debord's theorising of society as spectacle:

> Debord insists that spectacle is . . . the development of a technology of separation. It is the inevitable consequence of capitalism's 'restructuring of society without community' . . . It is in this sense that the management of attention, whether through early mass-cultural forms in the late nineteenth century or later through the television set or the computer monitor . . . has little to do with the visual content of these screens and far more with a larger strategy of the individual. Spectacle is not primarily concerned with looking at images but rather with the construction of conditions that individuate, immobilize, and separate subjects . . . In this way attention becomes key to the operation of noncoercive forms of power . . . Spectacle is not an optics of power but an architecture. Television and the personal computer . . . are methods for the management of attention . . . rendering bodies controllable and useful . . . even as they simulate the illusion of choices and 'interactivity' (Crary 2000: 73–5).

Foucault's reaction to Debord's *Society of the Spectacle* was largely dismissive: 'Our society,' he writes in *Discipline and Punish*, 'is not one of spectacle, but of surveillance . . . We are neither in the amphitheatre, nor on the stage, but in the panoptic machine' (1995: 217). For Foucault, the society of the spectacle—with its grand public displays of power and punishment—is an anachronism. As we saw in Chapter 3, he opens *Discipline and Punish* with a description of one such spectacle, the torture and execution of the regicide Robert-François Damiens in Paris in 1757, and explains how this kind of dramatic display had to go simply because it was often counter-productive. The Damiens affair is handled in a clumsy and ineffectual manner (for example, there are not enough horses to tear the body apart), and in the end power (the king, the state, justice) looks ridiculous and the crowd sympathises with the victim. Foucault argues that the society of the spectacle starts to disappear after the eighteenth century, and that power is increasingly exercised through surveillance. This culture of surveillance has been applied, literally and metaphorically, to populations from the nineteenth century up to the present. Moreover, Foucault's examples of the prison, the military academy, the school and the workplace as initial and obvious examples of disciplinary society can be succeeded, without much difficulty, by the notion of mass media and popular culture as sites of surveillance and self-surveillance.

Crary acknowledges 'Foucault's disdain, as he wrote one of the greatest meditations on modernity and power, for any facile . . . use of "spectacle" for an explanation of how the masses are . . . "duped" by media images' (2000: 18), but he points out that:

> Foucault's opposition of surveillance and spectacle seems to overlook how the effects of these two regimes of power can coincide. Using Bentham's panopticon as a primary theoretical object, Foucault relentlessly emphasizes the ways in which human subjects become objects of observation . . . but he neglects the new forms by which vision itself became a kind of discipline or mode of work . . . nineteenth-century optical devices . . . no less than the panopticon, involved arrangements of bodies in space, regulations of activity, and the deployment of individual bodies, which codified and normalized the observer within rigidly defined systems of visual consumption. They were techniques for the management of attention . . . The organization of mass culture . . . was fully embedded within the same transformations Foucault outlines (2000: 18).

Crary identifies four main aspects of the society of the spectacle. The first, and by far the most significant, concerns the task of attention management. Precisely because modern subjects have so many media and texts—visual and otherwise—addressing and attempting to engage them (such as audiovisual and poster advertising, radio jingles, computer emails, cell phone messages, digital sports scores, CD covers, book blurbs and covers, magazine photographs, newspaper headlines, and government and municipal signs), their attention span will necessarily be relatively brief. Spectacle and its sites and texts encourage this visual wanderlust ('never stop looking'), but at the same time spectacle needs to get results: the subject must be attentive enough for long enough to consume or comply. This is the second, related aspect of spectacle: 'vision is arranged, organised and disposed within various . . . visual regimes, the most influential and pervasive of which is capitalism' (Schirato 2007: 104). Third, every part and activity of socio-cultural life is made available for consumption and promoted as a commodity. They include both 'hard' (enlarged breasts and semi-permanent erections, replacement body parts, partners) and more affective commodity forms, which effectively are rolled into one (if you want to experience passion and identify with a group of people, buy a ticket to or watch a football game). Fourth, subjects experience and understand the world and themselves more or less exclusively through commodities and acts of consumption. At one level, this can be as straightforward as moving from one medium of information and entertainment to another to another ad infinitum: in the morning I read an online newspaper, get the weather and traffic forecasts from the radio, log into my computer at work, go home and watch television all night.

The conditions of spectacle, and the regimes of subjectivity that are consequent on it, are entirely consistent with the domination of the neo-liberal sensibilities and discourses that Foucault identifies and presages at the end of *The Birth of Biopolitics*. The media-as-spectacle inflects, and to some extent even transforms, practices and regimes of normalisation: in many socio-cultural contexts and spaces, the subject now relates to the self first and foremost as a commodity, and processes of normalisation function primarily within the logics and dictates of fashion and consumption. Making use of Arjun Appadurai's (1988) terminology, we can say that contemporary western subjectivity is largely situated within a commodity phase, meaning that its primary function, citation or orientation is that of exchange. This is what Foucault is moving towards when he refers, in *The Birth of Biopolitics*, to a 'theme-program of a society' and the 'optimization of systems of difference, in which minority individuals and practices are tolerated' (2008: 260). As Baudrillard (2003) points out, within late capitalist commodity culture difference is fetishised, because it facilitates the ongoing differentiation—and thus the potential commoditisation—of everything (fashion will eventually, for a short time, pass this way). The norm is now to differentiate oneself (just like everyone else), because this is the only marker of value. Applying Baudrillard's argument to the ideas expressed at the end of *The Birth of Biopolitics*, we can say that the culture of difference-as-value is the means by 'which action is brought to bear on the rules of the game rather than on the players, and finally in which there is an environmental type of intervention instead of the internal subjugation of individuals' (2008: 260).

Conclusion

Versions of the classical notion of the care of the self continue to reappear in western thought and animate discourses, practices and technologies of the self throughout the Christian and modern periods: Foucault refers to the Renaissance notion of the 'aesthetics of existence—the hero as his own work of art' (1997: 278)—and again to 'Nietzsche's observation in *The Gay Science* that one should create one's life by giving style to it through long practice and daily work' (1997: 262). Foucault also points out that the Stoic emphasis on the relation between self-care, rationality and the subject's position of duty with regard to the wider human community presages Kantian ethics. With Descartes and the rise of the human sciences, however, this rationality takes on an altogether different aspect. In Classical Greek thought, access to knowledge and truth is predicated upon the subject learning to take care of the self. In Stoic thought, the subject undergoes exercise in order to gain the autonomy, certainty and stability that reveals 'the order of the world as it stands' (1997: 279). With Descartes and the human sciences, evidence—or, more specifically, the ability to identify, analyse, evaluate and extrapolate from relevant data—is what is required to know the truth. Thus truth is effectively unmoored, not just from ascetic practices and care of the self but from any ethical or moral dimension. As Foucault writes:

> Before Descartes, one could not be impure, immoral, and know the truth. With Descartes, direct evidence is enough. After Descartes we have a nonascetic subject of knowledge. This change makes possible the institutionalization of modern science (1997: 279).

For Foucault, this development has foregrounded the problematical and difficult relation between knowledge, truth and ethics, an issue that was taken up by Kant, and more generally by what we can term the critical tradition in modern thought. 'Modern man,' Foucault writes, 'is the man who tries to invent himself. This modernity does not "liberate man in his own being"; it compels him to face the task of producing himself' (1980: 42). Foucault argues that critical thinking is the work we do in order to 'make' our subjectivity as an object of self-reflexive thought; and criticism in this sense is 'a historical investigation into the events that have led us to constitute ourselves and to recognise ourselves as subjects of what we are doing, thinking, saying' (1997: xxxv). These ideas will be explored in more detail in the next chapter.

6
~

Critique and ethics

Introduction

As we saw in Chapter 3, the reason of state required constant intervention in the lives of subjects-as-populations, which were dealt with and viewed in terms of principles and techniques of resource management. In order for the state to gain the maximum benefit from these resources, people had to be subjected to techniques that regulated and orientated thinking and general behaviour. This need produced what Foucault describes as 'a veritable explosion of the art of governing men' (2007b: 43).

Foucault argues that just as the imperative to govern, and the arts and techniques associated with and developed in accordance with it, were colonising socio-cultural fields, there was also a response that was highly contrary; he refers to this as extensive questions and considerations regarding 'how not to be governed' (2007b: 44). There was both an attitude of distrust and a concomitant determination to find ways and techniques of avoiding or limiting governing, which Foucault identifies as a precursor to what he refers to as the modern critical sensibility.

The Enlightenment as sensibility and politics

Foucault places the initial development of this critical sensibility in a specific time, place and set of circumstances—fifteenth- and sixteenth-century Western Europe, just prior to and during the Reformation. It is here, in this reaction to and against the spread of the reason of state and its apparatuses, logics, discourses and intrusions upon everyday life, that Foucault identifies the beginning of the Enlightenment as a reflexive, critical sensibility:

> if we accord this movement of governmentalization of both society and individuals the historic dimension and breadth which I believe it has had, it seems that one could approximately locate therein what we could call the critical attitude. Facing them head on and as compensation, or rather, as both partner and adversary to the arts of governing, as an act of defence, as . . . a way of limiting these arts of governing and . . . transforming them, of finding a way to escape from them or, in any case, a way to displace them, with a basic distrust . . . as a line of development of the arts of governing, there would be something born in Europe at that time, a kind of general cultural form, both a political and moral attitude . . . I would therefore propose, as a very first definition of critique, this general characterization: the art of not being governed quite so much (2007b: 44–5).

To what extent is the concept of critical inquiry continuous with regard to, and a necessary articulation of, the tendencies, claims, discourses and politics of the Enlightenment? Foucault makes clear his own refusal of what he terms 'the "blackmail" of the Enlightenment' and its 'doctrinal elements' (1997: 312). He characterises it as 'a set of political, economic, social, institutional, and cultural events on which we still depend in part', which constitutes:

a privileged domain for analysis. I also think that, as an enterprise for linking the progress of truth and the history of liberty . . . it formulated a philosophical question that remains for us to consider . . . Yet that does not mean one has to be 'for' or 'against' the Enlightenment. It means precisely that one must refuse everything that might present itself in the form of a simplistic and authoritarian alternative: you must either accept the Enlightenment and remain within the tradition of its rationalism . . . or else you criticize the Enlightenment and then try to escape from its principles of rationality (1997: 312–13).

The Enlightenment, as Foucault understands it, can be traced back to the development whereby human reason and rationality come to function as arbiters and mechanisms for determining truth and reality. This logic-as-praxis with which it is contemporaneous animates a specific conjunction of historical circumstances, forces and discourses encompassing the Renaissance, the Reformation, the emergence of science and the advent of humanism. Yet it is also at the centre of the development of imperatives commensurate with the reason of state, and its concomitant dispositions and techniques of surveillance and disciplinarity: Foucault's work testifies, for instance, to 'the importance acquired by scientific and technical rationality in the development of the productive forces and the play of political decisions' (Canguilhem 1991: 12). De Certeau (1988) writes about how, in a text such as *Discipline and Punish*, Foucault produces a story of the 'vampirisation' of the Enlightenment discourses of reason and rationality by the apparatuses, techniques and mechanisms that characterise, and provide the impetus for, the development of 'penetential, educational and medical control at the beginning of the nineteenth century' (1988: 45). For de Certeau, the relation between Enlightenment discourses and politics is not to be expressed as a dichotomy, but as a form of colonisation—disciplinary procedures take over the Enlightenment project, riding on the back of the ideology of revolution: 'All the while', de Certeau reminds us, 'ideology babbles on' (1988: 46).

There are a number of aspects of Foucault's work on disciplinary procedures—'This detective story about a substituted body' (de Certeau 1988: 46)—that are of particular interest here. First, although these procedures inhabit and feed off Enlightenment ideologies, they appear to have no discursive place of their own. Techniques that are neither derived from the *ancien régime*, nor explicable in terms of Enlightenment ideology, suddenly appear in a place, spreading themselves throughout social space to the extent that they, and not the contending notions and forces of revolution, triumph. How do such techniques and procedures establish themselves and proliferate without recourse to ideology or the authority of any specific regime of power? De Certeau looks for the answer in the Freudian narrative of the unconscious and the return of the repressed. Why do disciplinary techniques win out in the end? De Certeau suggests that:

> Through a cellular space of the same type for everyone (schoolboys, soldiers, workers, criminals or the ill), the techniques perfected the visibility and the gridwork of this space in order to make of it a tool capable of disciplining under control and 'treating' any human group whatsoever. The development is a matter of technological details, minuscule and decisive procedures (1988: 46).

What we have here is a testimony to the efficacy of a set of techniques of observation, regulation and discipline that will culminate in what is, for Foucault, our contemporary system of power, operating without regard to political authority or legitimation. But if such techniques have vampirised the Enlightenment project so successfully, it is because there is something in the conditions of the time and place that encourages their proliferation: the Enlightenment evacuates power from the place of the sovereign, and in its place sets up what Claude Lefort characterises (1988) as the 'empty space' of democracy, in which power is not tied to any specific content. The question remains, however, of just how the state is to function (for instance, how is a population to be organised, educated, controlled?) without recourse to sovereignty. In a sense, the evacuation of the place of power (power understood as a 'without regard to') can also be understood as an invitation to the concealment of power. This other side of the Enlightenment 'inverts revolutionary institutions from within and establishes everywhere the "penitentiary" in place of penal justice' (1988: 46).

The Enlightenment as critical attitude

In the essays 'What is Enlightenment?' (1997) and 'What is Critique?' (2007b), Foucault focuses on 'a more positive content', explaining how his work could be considered to have affinities with the Enlightenment project. In his discussion, in 'What is Enlightenment?', of the relation between Enlightenment and what he calls 'the attitude of modernity' (1997: 311), Foucault describes the Enlightenment as a historically grounded event (characterised by various activities, discourses, institutions, politics and forms of knowledge) that is simultaneously 'a philosophical ethos that could be described as a permanent critique of our historical era' (1997: 312). This attitude is not just directed at, nor does it exhaust its work with regard to, the social, cultural and historical regimes that constitute the world of the subject; rather, those contexts—limited, limiting and changeable as they are—are the departure points for a process whereby the subject critiques what it says, thinks and does (1997: 315), and takes itself 'as object of a complex and difficult elaboration' (1997: 311).

Foucault identifies certain concepts and characteristics that both constitute the basis of Enlightenment for Kant, and also strongly inform his own work. The most important of these is the recognition of difference: for Kant, identifying change or movement in contemporary reality provides a 'way out' (1997: 305) whereby we can exercise our reason with regard to the workings of authority, power and meaning. How does this happen? The 'way out' of Enlightenment is to be understood, first, as an ability and willingness to utilise reason in order to come to a knowledge of reality (that is, understanding how the everyday world is organised so that the contingent is disguised as and takes on the status of the universal); and second, as an imperative to disseminate that knowledge to the public at large.

In 'What is Critique?', Foucault suggests that the Enlightenment project, forced to deal with the politics of 'humanity in the minority condition', makes use of a critical sensibility to 'lift this minority condition and in some way majoritize men' (2007b: 48). This is an important point for Foucault, and one that must be taken into account when considering both the turn to an apparent 'personalised aesthetics' of his later books (the last two volumes of *The History of Sexuality*) and the strong emphasis that is placed, in the various lecture series recorded in the 1980s, on the principle that one's personal ethos functions as the form and marker of an exemplary politics. He writes that, for Kant, the Enlightenment is 'a distinctive feature by which one can be recognised, and it is also a motto, an instruction that one gives oneself and proposes to others', and therefore 'must be considered both as a process in which men participate collectively and an act of courage to be accomplished personally' (1997: 306).

We can say, in summary, that Foucault associates critique with five main characteristics. First, it is relational, being a response to something other than itself (power, social doxa, the limits of thought). Second, the form it takes is historically specific, so the modern version of critique (as a reaction against being governed at a micro level) differs markedly from, while having its origins and antecedents in, Medieval Christianity and, even further removed, Classical Greece and the Hellenistic world (2007b: 42). Third, it is heterogeneous and 'condemned to dispersion' (2007b: 42), and incapable of instituting or establishing itself as a regime of socio-cultural practice or an author-ised form of knowledge (akin to philosophy, politics and law), except in the most limited way. Fourth, it is not exhausted by or reducible to what Foucault refers to as 'the stiff bit of utility' (2007b: 42): above and beyond its formal functions—the reduction of error, the testing of epistemological parameters—there is 'something in critique which is akin to virtue' (2007b: 43). Fifth and finally, this 'something akin to virtue' has an ethical dimension, related to the Enlightenment duty of ensuring that 'the use of reason can take the public form that it requires' (1997: 308).

Critique and ethics

How does Foucault understand critique as a form of ethical behav-iour? In the field of philosophy, the term 'ethics' usually refers to the 'standards by which a particular group or community decides to regu-late its behaviour—to distinguish what is legitimate . . . in pursuit of their aims from what is not' (Flew 1983: 112). Philosophy also distin-guishes between normative ethics, understood as a specific content and set of imperatives or directions that regulate or dispose how a community conducts itself, and meta-ethics, which refers more gener-ally to questions regarding 'the logical form of morality' (1983: 114). Foucault defines morality as 'a set of values and rules of action that are recommended to individuals through the intermediary of various prescriptive agencies such as the family . . . educational institutions, churches, and so forth' (1985: 25). Morality also refers to the extent to which there is an articulation from a moral code (the rules) to indi-vidual or group practices (1985: 26).

Foucault is particularly interested in a third form of morality, however: the extent to which the relation between code and practice constitutes the context of, and departure point for, the formation of the subject's relation to oneself as ethos:

For a rule of conduct is one thing; the conduct that may be measured by this rule is another. But another thing still is the manner in which one ought to 'conduct oneself'—that is, the manner in which one ought to form oneself as an ethical subject acting in reference to the prescriptive elements that make up the code. Given a code of actions (which can be defined by their degree of conformity with or divergence from the code), there are always ways to 'conduct oneself' morally, different ways for the acting individual to operate, not just as an agent, but as the ethical subject of this action (1985: 26).

The example that Foucault gives in *The Use of Pleasure* is the way in which the notion of sexual 'fidelity' might be the site of what he calls the 'determination of the ethical substance' (1985: 26). In an obvious sense, fidelity can function simply as a rule that must be observed and lived (one has sexual activity only with a single partner); but it can also be a negative—for instance, as the scene of a more general agonistics with the self (as in Christianity, where fidelity is primarily understood as an aspect of the denial of the flesh that leads to spiritual self-transformation); or again, it can have the opposite emphasis, standing in for or manifesting the emotion or feeling (intensity of passion, attraction, love, devotion) that guarantees the authenticity of a relationship.

These differences are differentiated further by what Foucault refers to as the mode of subjectivity (say, how one's identity as the member of a wider social, religious or political community relates and gives meaning to practices of sexual abstention); the forms of elaboration of the ethical work (for instance, regimes of learning, discipline and self-surveillance that enable the subject to meet the challenges of the flesh); and the telos of the ethical subject (fidelity might be a stage in the process of self-mastery). For Foucault, morality is not reducible to the law, a rule or a regime of conduct. All moral action involves both:

a relationship with the reality in which it is carried out, and a relationship with the self. The latter is not simply 'self-awareness' but self-formation as an 'ethical subject', a process in which the individual delimits that part of himself that will form the object of the moral practice, defines his position relative to the precept he will follow, and decides on a certain mode of being that will serve as his moral goal. And this requires him to act upon himself, to monitor, test, improve, and transform himself. There is no specific moral action that does not refer to a unified moral conduct; no moral conduct that does not call for the forming of oneself as an ethical subject . . . Moral actions are indissociable from . . . forms of self-activity, and they do not differ any less from one morality to another than do the systems of values, rules, and interdictions (1985: 28).

Here, Foucault is distinguishing between ethics as (adherence to) a system and set of roles understood as a form of universality (and therefore largely ahistorical and non-specific) on the one hand, and as a set of negotiated practices and specificities (of dispositions, durations, relations, techniques) that is both historical (it is embedded in time and place) and continuous (it requires and constitutes a work that must always be returned to) on the other. The nub of this differentiation is the role or form of work allocated the subject: in the former, the subject predominantly reproduces a content that is prescribed and derived from elsewhere, while the latter approximates more closely to what Foucault (1986) refers to as 'the care of the self'.

As Arnold Davidson points out in his introduction to the group of lectures collected in *The Hermeneutics of the Subject* (2005), this distinction more or less parallels Foucault's notion of the Enlightenment as both doctrine and attitude. What Foucault calls ethics is simultaneously commensurate with and derived from bodies of knowledge (the human sciences) that simultaneously explain and prescribe the truth of the world. It is a reflexive disposition, involving the permanent 'testing of oneself, of one's mode of being and thought' in the form of 'an historical-practical test of the limits that we can go beyond . . . the work of ourselves on ourselves as free beings' (2005: xxvii). The 'slow, sustained, and arduous work' (2005: xvii) that characterises both the Enlightenment-as-attitude and the disposition and practices of the ethical subject is oriented towards opening up or making a space for the possibility of thinking otherwise; this is Kant's 'way out' from contemporary reality, where we are able to 'detach ourselves from the already given systems, orders, doctrines, and codes of philosophy' (2005: xxvii). For Foucault, this detachment-as-freedom constitutes 'the ontological condition of ethics' (1997: 284): it allows the subject to move from a position whereby systems and doctrines of thought prescribe, stand in for and guarantee truth (including the conditions, meanings and telos of the subject's own life) to one where they are assigned the status of discursive players in the 'games of truth and error through which being is historically constituted as experience; that is, as something that can and must be thought' (1985: 6–7).

Games of truth, for Foucault, are the discursive conditions and parameters—the categories, narratives, exemplifications, norms and explanations—that both enable and determine the 'between us' of the subject's relation to both the wider socio-cultural field and the self. They are universal in the sense that they self-authorise themselves as such: this is achieved by foreclosing or rendering as abject other alternatives; by effectively concealing or disappearing the conditions of their own emergence; and by disguising or transforming arbitrariness or particularity as universal, ahistorical and natural. The identification of the gap that is opened up between claims of universality and particular interests (which are framed as universal) constitutes the conditions for the emergence of the 'way out' of critical thinking and questioning. This questioning, however, is enacted by subjects who themselves are necessarily within, and products of, the world of norms and discursive regimes and distinct cultural fields.

The ethical disposition to which Foucault refers is tied to the question of how subjects can become reflective about or attain a reflexive relation with regard to themselves, their utterances and the conditions under which such utterances are made possible. Foucault insists that the operations and effects of power are productive as well as restrictive. He posits three conditions or contexts that produce, and allow the subject to achieve, some level of reflexivity. First, the distinctions, definitions and differentiations of disciplinary apparatuses and discourses produce categories and subject positions (anti-subjects, non-subjects, delinquent subjects) that are antithetical to the procedures and regimes of normalisation; as we saw in our previous chapter, the normal and the human are always inhabited by, and constituted from, an excess or remainder, something outside the limits of the subject. Second, the changes to, and the often erratic trajectories of, norms across time and place point to the particularity and arbitrariness of that which claims to be universal—there is always a heterogeneity of historical forms and manifestations of the supposedly homogeneous, timeless and ahistorical. Third, and perhaps most importantly, the subject is not simply or necessarily an effect of discourse: Foucault identifies a process or logic whereby what he calls the 'critical attitude' (2007b) arises out of the creation, dissemination and deployment of those (historically specific) ideas, imperatives and dispositions that come to constitute or contribute to a particular grid of intelligibility.

The process to which Foucault refers and that he describes is intensively technical, to the extent that the question of agency is subordinate to that of literacy. Moreover, this kind of intensive and highly literate regime is inexplicable without reference to a set of contexts that make available, authorise, teach, facilitate, reinforce and naturalise what is effectively a reflexive and critical disposition and praxis. If this is a form of agency, it is one made available through and as part of what Pierre Bourdieu (2000) calls a habitus (1991), and it requires a more detailed explanation of how 'all moral action involves a relationship with the reality in which it is carried out' (Foucault 1985: 28).

As Bourdieu (2000) demonstrates, subjects are in the world

because the world is in them—that is, sustained membership of any cultural field, including the wider field of the social, is predicated on both a literacy with regard to, and an appropriate performance of, its principles, values, templates and cultural imperatives. Every cultural field is not only made up from and through its own discourses, but also by distinctive genres and forms of address. Social activities and performances are characterised by highly conventionalised, and even ritualised, embodied codes that determine how and when one articulates an account of oneself (with regard to tone, discourse and pace), and the kinds of narratives that one can address to different subject categories (based, for instance, on gender, social standing and age). Moreover, these conditions of address are themselves subject to time, and therefore not stable: the account that is facilitated, inflected or directed by one place or context will be replaced by something emanating from marginally or entirely different configurations of subject position and cultural field.

For Foucault, the norms and discourses that characterise a particular discursive regime also constitute the subject who questions, and so to question norms is to bring into jeopardy the truth and sustainability of the self. Subjects are recognised and accepted as long as they perform in accordance with the rules, logics, imperatives, values and discourses—that is, the norms—of society. At the same time, there are cultural fields where taking a reflexive attitude to the conditions of one's subjectivity is not only something towards which one is disposed; it can also constitute a means by which a subject attains capital, and/or it can be recognised as the condition by which the subject lives out and in accordance with the ethos of the field. To think in a reflexive manner involves, first and foremost, learning to think at and through limits that are themselves constitutive of how we come to see, categorise, understand and relate to the world and to ourselves. Reflexivity, from this perspective, is not quite the same as critique, but it can be seen as the part of critique that, in Foucault's terms, is charged with 'eradicating errors' (2007b: 42–3).

To summarise, we can say that, for Foucault, an ethical praxis has five main features. First, it is not reducible to the idea of a rule—it is not simply a compliant response to what is already mandatory, whether in the form of a precept, injunction or law. Second, it involves a process of taking and delimiting oneself as an object of self-formation and ongoing transformation. Third, it requires not only thinking through, but also an examination, monitoring and testing of, the self in relation to the wider context of the socio-cultural world (and its rules, forms of value, narratives and imperatives). Fourth, this testing of the self takes place via a comparison between a seemingly self-formulated code of conduct (a discourse) and a set or pattern of behaviour (a praxis). Fifth, this process of self-testing and self-formulation constitutes, and is itself constituted as, a reflex.

Parrhesia and truth-telling

The notion of critique is increasingly understood, in Foucault's later work, as an aspect of the problem of the ethics, pragmatics and techniques of truth-telling. The issue of what is at stake in, and the limits and conditions of, the public form of speech is central to this later work, particularly the last two volumes of *The History of Sexuality*, and the essays, lectures, talks and interviews collected in volumes such as *Fearless Speech* (2001), *The Hermeneutics of the Subject* (2005) and *The Politics of Truth* (2007b). Butler suggests that for Foucault, in giving an account of oneself:

> one is also exhibiting, in the very speech that one uses, the logos by which one lives. The point is not only to bring speech into accord with action . . . it is also to acknowledge that speaking is already a kind of doing, a form of action, one that is already a moral practice and a way of life (2005: 126).

Foucault devotes the lectures collected in *Fearless Speech* to an analysis and consideration of the Greek concept of *parrhesia* or 'free speech', which can be dated to the fifth century BC and is still found in use—having evolved in meaning across Greek and Roman culture—eight centuries later (2001: 11). *Parrhesia* refers both to a type of content (the parrhesiastes provides a full and candid account of the subject's thoughts and opinions on a particular matter), and a form of relationship (the purpose is not to use rhetorical devices to persuade, but rather to demonstrate to interlocutors that there is a corollary between one's words and one's beliefs and actions). Foucault distinguishes two major forms of *parrhesia*. One form is pejorative, is often found in anti-democratic and Christian contexts, and refers to a situation where someone speaks without sense or thought. The other form, most frequently found in Classical texts, is associated with truthfulness:

> To my mind, the parrhesiates says what is true because he knows that it is really true. The parrhesiastes is not only sincere and says what is his opinion, but his opinion is also the truth. He says what he knows to be true. The second characteristic of *parrhesia*, then, is that there is always an exact coincidence between belief and truth (2001: 14).

How can one be sure of 'an exact coincidence' between one's opinion or belief, what one says and the truth? This question is not just an abstraction: it emerges, more overtly and insistently, in specific cultural fields and across a wider society when the accounts and discourses that subjects, institutions and communities use to 'speak or show themselves' become the object of analysis—much as when, in Kuhnian terms, a particular paradigm turns its analytical gaze increasingly upon itself (Kuhn 1970). In asking or posing this question, Foucault is focusing attention on one particular historical context and its issues of truth-telling in order to gain an understanding of both the emergence of the notion of critical thinking and, as a corollary, the contemporary relationship between subjectivity and the operations of power. 'Relinking truth-telling to the problem of power,' Foucault remarks:

> in the fifth century BC philosophical problems emerged in relation to questions about the allocation of power: Who is able to tell the truth, about what, with what consequences, and with what relation to power? Although truth-telling is compelled to proceed according to rules of validity, Foucault also makes clear that there are conditions—I would call them rhetorical—that make truth-telling possible and must be interrogated. In this sense, the problematization of truth must take into account 'the importance of telling the truth, knowing who is able to tell the truth, and knowing why we should tell the truth' (Butler 2005: 131).

The parrhesiastes is always involved in telling the truth to an audience, whether it is a communal assembly, a friend or the ruler of a city, in order to effect a change of some kind. The audience needs both to comprehend the truth and be moved by it; such a scene is potentially a 'social occasion for self-transformation' (Butler 2005: 130). *Parrhesia* constitutes a critical attitude directed at a form of behaviour, attitude or set of beliefs that stands in the way of the subject's duty. In making this criticism, the parrhesiastes will often point to their own experience and fallibilities; *parrhesia* can be directed at another or oneself. The duty that the parrhesiastes is required to perform, first and foremost, is tied to *parrhesia* itself: it is to facilitate, circulate and demonstrate the truth.

What guarantees *parrhesia*? What authorises it, testifies to it, demonstrates it? To deal with these questions, we need to return to and reconsider the issue of what is at stake in telling the truth for the parrhesiates. We had suggested that what was at stake was doing one's duty, but that answer can seem both rhetorical and circular. We can, by way of exemplification, digress here and refer to Slavoj Žižek's (1996) analysis of what is, and isn't, at stake in virtual subjectivities played out through internet chatrooms, games and communities such as *Second Life*:

> The problem of communication in virtual communities is thus not simply that I can lie (that an ugly old man can present himself as a beautiful young woman, etc.) but, more fundamentally, that I am never truly engaged, since at any moment I can pull back, unhook myself. In virtual community sex games I can be ruthless, I can pour out all my dirty dreams, precisely because my word no longer obliges me, is not 'subjectivized' (1996: 196).

When Žižek refers to engagement as a precondition of being subjectivised, he is pointing to something that Foucault understands as being constitutive of *parrhesia*: there are consequences of identifying with or speaking from a subject position—or for that matter and more commonly, being identified through being called the name of a subject category. For Foucault, the doubt as to whether one is a parrhesiates, and what we would call the proof of the authenticity and reliability of the *parrhesia*, is both given in and guaranteed by the 'moral qualities' (2001: 15) of the speaker. As Foucault writes, the 'parrhesiastic game' presupposes qualities that are 'required to know the truth . . . and . . . convey such truth to others' (2001: 15).

The notion of *parrhesia* as a game refers to the relationship into which the parrhesiastes enters, an exchange played out between interlocutors utilising an agreed set of rules or conventions, and in which something is being played for or is at stake. One important rule, according to Foucault, is that the parrhesiastes is not only frank, but there is also (and necessarily) 'a risk or danger for him in telling the truth' (2001: 16). This is because the parrhesiastes directs a form of criticism while being 'in a position of inferiority with respect to the interlocutor' (2001: 18). The position of inferiority is, of course, understood in terms of having access to power of some kind. So when a parrhesiastes rebukes an assembly or majority opinion, there is a risk of a backlash, unpopularity and in some instances physical injury or (in the case of Socrates) death. To speak from a position where the interlocutor is in one's power is not an instance of *parrhesia*, for there is little or nothing at risk. This returns us to the issue of the moral qualities that characterise the parrhesiastes. Putting oneself in danger because of the necessity of speaking the truth, and the consistency with which one does one's duty despite the possibility of injury or annihilation or alienation (in Classical Athens, unpopular speakers could and were ostracised), guarantees and embodies the truth that one speaks understood as the truth of the self:

> When you accept the parrhesiastic game in which your own life is exposed, you are taking up a specific relationship to yourself: you risk death to tell the truth instead of reposing in the security of a life where the truth goes unspoken. Of course, the threat of death comes from the Other, and thereby requires a relationship to the Other. But the parrhesiastes primarily chooses a specific relationship to himself: he prefers himself as a truth-teller rather than as a living being who is false to himself (2001: 17).

In the course of his negotiation of the issues at hand—he is considering what is the point of, or what is at stake in, this line of inquiry—Foucault refers to the ways in which *parrhesia* constitutes the site or locus of various problematics, largely in terms of what we might term their technical aspects (What distinguishes a parrhesias-tes or truth teller? How can we 'know' what is authentic *parrhesia*?). However, he is also taking into account 'the problem of truth' (2001:

73). *Parrhesia*-as-problem comes to exemplify and manifest a more general notion of epistemological crisis, transformation or change. As Foucault makes clear, at a local and specific time and place, *parrhesia* initially takes on or is associated with a series of relatively consistent meanings (the parrhesiates tells all, speaks fearlessly, confronts power) that gradually become problematical—so, for example, as Athenian democracy at the end of the fifth century is corrupted and destabilised by demagoguery, and consequently suffers military reversals and disasters in the Peloponnesian War, this brings into focus the problem 'of recognizing who is capable of speaking the truth within the limits of an institutional system where everyone is entitled to give their opinion' (2001: 73). At this point, Foucault articulates the significance of the notion of problematisation to his work and thought:

I emphasize this point for at least the following methodological reasons. I would like to distinguish between the 'history of ideas' and the 'history of thought'. Most of the time a historian of ideas tries to determine when a specific concept appears, and this moment is often identified by the appearance of a new word. But what I am attempting to do as an historian is something different. I am trying to analyze the way institutions, practices, habits, and behavior become a problem for people who behave in specific sorts of ways, who have certain types of habits, who engage in certain kinds of practices, and who put to work specific kinds of institutions . . . The history of thought is the analysis of the way an unproblematic field of experience, or a set of practices, which were accepted without question, which were familiar and 'silent' . . . becomes a problem . . . and induces a crisis . . . The history of thought . . . is the history of the way people begin to take care of something, of the way they become anxious about this or that—for example, about madness, about crime, about sex, about themselves, or about truth (2001: 74).

Conclusion

Parrhesia is a significant concept for Foucault because it is a site that functions as a locus of meaning-as-power, where the relation between various socio-cultural institutions, concepts, meanings, genres and practices (the people as government, freedom, duty, public speech) is rethought and negotiated in a moment of crisis, in the process demanding 'a new way of taking care of and asking questions about these relations' (2001: 74). It serves as an example of a 'problematic field of experience' that produces thinking, activity and meaning that can no longer be taken for granted—in other words, it is a site where thought and meaning have temporarily become unmoored, with all the accompanying consequences. The silence that accompanies the normal and natural here gives way to an anxiety and concomitant speech that is trying to 'take care of something'—whether it be the notion of truth, the parameters of socio-cultural duty, or more generally the various accounts cultures give of themselves. In a general methodological sense, Foucault traces, describes and analyses the history of the discourses, meanings and accounts that emanate from specific socio-cultural and temporal intersection, each one a specific 'answer of thought . . . to a certain situation' (2001: 173). So in place of those methods of scholarship and research (historical, philosophical, psychoanalytical, linguistic) that seek to identify 'formal structures with universal value' (Foucault 1997: 315), Foucault focuses on 'the events that have led us to constitute ourselves and to recognize ourselves as subjects of what we are doing, thinking, saying' (1997: 315).

Problematisation is derived from two methodologies utilised by Foucault: archaeology and genealogy. They have been referred to, defined and exemplified in other chapters, but for our present purposes we need to emphasise that archaeology identifies structures of meaning as events whereby local and temporal narratives, genres, bodies of knowledge and discursive regimes are effectively universalised; and genealogy 'separates out, from the contingency that has made us what we are' (1997: 315) the possibility of being or doing otherwise. As Foucault makes clear, this is methodology employed for the purposes of critical inquiry informed by a specific sensibility and ethos, undertaking what he calls 'the undefined work of freedom' (1997: 316). Critical inquiry is directed at the limitations of thought that are constitutive of thought—with the aim of producing freedom from the 'limits of ourselves' (1997: 316). This is not a universal and universalising project: the space opened up by critical inquiry must always 'put itself to the test of reality, both to grasp the points where change is possible and desirable, and to determine the precise form this change should take' (1997: 316).

Bibliography

Foucault's works

Foucault, M (1972) *The Archaeology of Knowledge*, trans A Sheridan Smith. Tavistock, New York. First published 1969 as *L'archéologie du savoir*, Gallimard, Paris.

—— (1973) *The Order of Things: An Archaeology of the Human Sciences*, Vintage, New York. First published 1966 as *Les mots et les choses—une archéologie des sciences humaines*, Gallimard, Paris.

—— (1975) *Birth of the Clinic: An Archaeology of Medical Perception*, trans A Sheridan Smith. Vintage, New York. First published 1963 as *Naissance de la clinique—une archéologie du regard medical*, PUF, Paris.

—— (1978) *The History of Sexuality: Volume 1—An Introduction*, trans R Hurley. Penguin, Harmondsworth. First published 1976 as *Histoire de la sexualité: Vol I: La Volonté de savoir*, Gallimard, Paris.

—— (1980) *Power/Knowledge: Selected Interviews and Other Writings*, ed C Gordon. Pantheon, New York.

—— (1982) *I, Pierre Riviere*. University of Nebraska Press, Lincoln,

NE. First published 1973 as *Moi, Pierre Rivière, ayant égorgé ma mère, ma soeur et mon frère*, Gallimard, Paris.

—— (1985) *The History of Sexuality: Volume 2—The Use of Pleasure*, trans R Hurley. Penguin, Harmondsworth. First published 1984 as *Histoire de la sexualité, Vol II: L'Usage des plaisirs*, Gallimard, Paris.

—— (1986a) *The History of Sexuality: Volume 3—The Care of the Self*, trans R Hurley. Penguin, Harmondsworth. First published 1984 as *Histoire de la sexualité, Vol III: Le Souci de soi*, Gallimard, Paris.

—— (1986b) 'Nietzsche, Genealogy, History', in M Foucault, *Language, Counter-Memory, Practice*, D Bouchard (ed). Cornell University Press, Ithaca, NY.

—— (1988a) *Madness and Civilization: A History of Insanity in the Age of Reason*, trans R Howard. Tavistock, London. First published 1961 as *Histoire de la folie à l'âge classique—Folie et de raison*, Plon, Paris.

—— (1988b) *Politics, Philosophy, Culture: Interviews and Other Writings, 1977–1984*, trans A Sheridan, ed L Kritzman. Routledge, London.

—— (1991) *The Foucault Reader*, ed P Rabinow. Penguin, Harmondsworth.

—— (1995) *Discipline and Punish: The Birth of the Prison*, trans A Sheridan. Vintage, New York. First published 1975 as *Surveiller et punir*, Gallimard, Paris.

—— (1997) *Ethics: Essential Works 1954–1984*, Volume 1, trans R Hurley, ed P Rabinow. Penguin, Harmondsworth.

—— (1998) *Aesthetics, Method, and Epistemology: Essential Works 1954–84*, Volume 2, trans R Hurley, ed P Rabinow. New Press, New York.

—— (2000) *Power: Essential Works 1954–84*, Volume 3, trans R Hurley, ed P Rabinow. New Press, New York.

—— (2001) *Fearless Speech*. Semiotext(e), Los Angeles.

—— (2003a) *Abnormal: Lectures at the Collège de France 1974–75*, trans G Burchell. Picador, New York. First published 1999 as *Les anormaux: Cours au Collège de France 1974–5*, Seuil, Paris.

—— (2003b) *Society Must Be Defended: Lectures at the Collège de France 1975–76*, trans D Macey. Penguin, Harmondsworth. First published 1997 as *Il faut défendre la société*, Gallimard & Seuil, Paris.

—— (2005) *The Hermeneutics of the Subject: Lectures at the Collège de France 1982–83*, trans G Burchell. Picador, New York. First published 2001 as *L'hermeneutique du sujet: Cours au Collège de France 1981–1982*, Seuil, Paris.

—— (2006a) *Psychiatric Power: Lectures at the Collège de France 1973–74*, trans G Burchell. Palgrave Macmillan, Basingstoke. First published 2003 as *Le Pouvoir psychiatrique: Cours au Collège de France 1973–1974*, Seuil, Paris.

—— (2006b) *History of Madness*, trans J Murphy and J Khalfa. Routledge, New York. First published 1961 as *Histoire de la folie à l'âge classique—Folie et déraison*, Plon, Paris.

—— (2007a) *Security, Territory, Population: Lectures at the Collège de France 1977–78*, trans G Burchell. Palgrave Macmillan, Basingstoke. First published 2004 as *Sécurité, territoire, population: Cours au Collège de France 1977–1978*, Seuil, Paris.

—— (2007b) *The Politics of Truth*, trans L Hochroch and C Porter. Semiotext(e), Los Angeles.

—— (2008) *The Birth of Biopolitics: Lectures at the Collège de France 1978–79*, trans G Burchell. Palgrave Macmillan, Basingstoke. First published 2004 as *Naissance de la biopolitique: Cours au Collège de France 1978–1979*, Seuil, Paris.

—— (2010) *The Government of Self and Others: Lectures at the Collège de France 1982–83*, trans G Burchell. Palgrave Macmillan, Basingstoke. First published 2008 as *Le gouvernement de soi et des autres: Cours au Collège de France 1982–1983*, Seuil, Paris.

Other works

Agamben, G (2009) *What is an Apparatus? And Other Essays*. Stanford University Press, Stanford, CA.

American Psychiatric Association (APA) (2011) *Diagnostic and Statistical Manual of Mental Disorders*, Volume 4. APA, Washington, DC. Retrieved 23 March 2011 from <www.psyweb.com/dsm_iv/isp/dsm_iv.jsp>.

Appadurai, A (1988) *The Social Life of Things*. Cambridge University Press, Cambridge.

Baudrillard, J (2003) *The Consumer Society*, trans G Ritzer. Sage, London.

Bourdieu, P (1990) *In Other Words*, trans M Adamson. Polity Press, Cambridge.

—— (1991) *Language and Symbolic Power*, trans M Adamson and G Raymond. Harvard University Press, Cambridge, MA.

—— (2000) *Pascalian Meditations*, trans R Nice. Polity Press, Cambridge.

Bourdieu, P and Eagleton T (1984) 'Doxa and Common Life: An Interview', in S Žižek (ed), *Mapping Ideology*. Verso, London.

Butler, J (1990) *Gender Trouble*. Routledge, New York.

—— (1993) *Bodies That Matter*. Routledge, New York.

—— (2005) *Giving an Account of Oneself*. Fordham University Press, New York.

Canguilhem, G (1991) *The Normal and the Pathological*, trans C Fawcett. C Zone Books, New York.

Catton, E (2009) *The Rehearsal*. Victoria University Press, Wellington, NZ.

Chomsky, N and Foucault, M (2006) *The Chomsky–Foucault Debate: On Human Nature*. New Press, New York.

Crary, J (1998) *Techniques of the Observer*. MIT Press, Cambridge, MA.

—— (2000) *Suspensions of Perception*. MIT Press, Cambridge, MA.

De Certeau, M (1984) *The Practice of Everyday Life*, trans S Rendall. University of California Press, Berkeley, CA.

—— (1986) *Heterologies: Discourse on the Other*, trans B Massumi. University of Minnesota Press, Minneapolis, MN.

—— (1988) *The Writing of History*, trans T Conley. Columbia University Press, New York.

Deleuze, G and Guattari, F (1972) *Anti-Oedipus*, trans R Hurley, M Seem and H Lane. Continuum, London.

Dreyfus, H and Rabinow, P (1986) *Michel Foucault: Beyond Structuralism and Hermeneutics*. Harvester, Brighton.

Flew, T (1983) *Ethics and Public Policy*, Prentice-Hall, Englewood Cliffs, NJ.

Frow, J (2005) *Genre*, Routledge, London.

Fukuyama, F (1992) *The End of History and the Last Man*. Free Press, New York.

Kipling, R (1929) 'The White Man's Burden: The United States & The Philippine Islands, 1899', in *Rudyard Kipling's Verse: Definitive Edition*. Doubleday, New York.

Kuhn, T (1970) *The Structure of Scientific Revolutions*. University of Chicago Press, Chicago.

Leahy, D (2010) 'What's On (or Off) the Menu in School?' *Text*, Special Issue, no 9.

Lefort, C (1986) *The Political Forms of Modern Society*. MIT Press, Cambridge, MA.

Lodge, D (1988) *Nice Work*. Penguin, London.

Mattelart, A (1994) *Mapping World Communication*. University of Minnesota Press, Minneapolis, MN.

—— (2000) *Networking the World: 1794–2000*, trans L Carey-Libbrecht and J Cohen. University of Minnesota Press, Minneapolis, MN.

—— (2003) *The Information Society*. Sage, London.

McNay, L (1994) *Foucault: A Critical Introduction*. Continuum, New York.

Nietzsche, F (1956) *The Birth of Tragedy and the Genealogy of Morals*, trans F Golffing, Doubleday, New York.

Said, E (1978) *Orientalism*. Penguin, London.

—— (1984) *The World, the Text, and the Critic*. Faber & Faber, London.

Schirato, T (2007) *Understanding Sports Culture*. Sage, London.

Schirato, T and Webb, J (2003) *Understanding Globalization*. Sage, London.

—— (2004) *Understanding the Visual*. Sage, London.

Virilio, P (1991) *The Lost Dimension*, trans D Moshenberg. Semiotext(e), New York.

Wikipedia (2011) 'Mammal'. Retrieved 22 March 2011 from <http://en.wikipedia.org/wiki/Mammal>.

World Health Organization (WHO) (2003) *Diet, Nutrition and the Prevention of Chronic Diseases*, Technical Report Series no. 916, WHO, Geneva. Retrieved 21 July 2011 from <www.who.int/nutrition/publications/obesity/WHO_TRS_916/en/index.html>.

Žižek, S (1991) *For They Know Not What They Do*. Verso, London.

—— (1996) *The Indivisible Remainder: Essays on Schelling and Related Matters*. Verso, London.

Index